W9-AQN-739

# TESTAMENT OF A CRITIC

# Books by George Jean Nathan

THE AUTOBIOGRAPHY OF AN ATTITUDE
ART OF THE NIGHT · THE HOUSE OF SATAN
LAND OF THE PILGRIMS' PRIDE
THE NEW AMERICAN CREDO · MONKS ARE MONKS
A BOOK WITHOUT A TITLE
MATERIA CRITICA · THE POPULAR THEATRE
MR. GEORGE JEAN NATHAN PRESENTS
THE THEATRE, THE DRAMA, THE GIRLS
ANOTHER BOOK ON THE THEATRE
COMEDIANS ALL · THE WORLD IN FALSEFACE
THE CRITIC AND THE DRAMA

*In Collaboration with H. L. Mencken*
EUROPE AFTER 8:15 · HELIOGABALUS
THE AMERICAN CREDO

*Books on George Jean Nathan*
THE QUINTESSENCE OF NATHANISM,
*by Vladimar Kozlenko*
THE THEATRE OF GEORGE JEAN NATHAN
*by Isaac Goldberg, Ph.D.*

ALFRED·A·KNOPF
*NEW YORK* 1931 *LONDON*

# TESTAMENT *of a* CRITIC

*GEORGE JEAN NATHAN*

ALFRED · A · KNOPF

*NEW YORK*    1931    *LONDON*

PN2266
N37

# CONTENTS

# TESTAMENT OF A
## CRITIC

# BOOK I : REVELATION

"*A Beast Riseth Out of the Sea.*"—In the exposition of what I myself happen to believe, it is certainly not my purpose to argue or even to hint that this personal set of beliefs is either philosophically or emotionally admirable or that its adoption by anyone else is a consummation devoutly wished on my part. I suspect that what other men believe, though it be often objectionable to me, may stand them in quite as sound service as my own beliefs stand me, and that it may contribute equally to their self-esteem, happiness, bank accounts, worldly eminence and wives' low opinion of them. A man's beliefs, after all, save he be a professional practitioner of letters and hence a racketeer of words, a self-blackmailer and a Judas unto himself, are and should be his private, personal property, as safe from vulgar public scrutiny as his underwear. There is something indelicate, even bounderish, in exposing one's most secret articles of faith, a fact appreciated by the relatively gentlemanly among the professional carpenters of letters mentioned, as may be witnessed by the obvious posturings, evasions and mendacities they indulge in when they engage, for

3

hire, to contribute to the public prints. There is about the "beliefs" they expound on such occasions a considerable air of fraud; it is plain that, while they are ostensibly betraying their confidences, they are withholding much that is true of themselves and of their private philosophies, and much that, being true, would be altogether too embarrassing to set down in print. By way of subterfuge, they accordingly offer to the public a bold, forthright, cocksure and impudent front — but with their fingers carefully crossed behind their backs. If we may put any trust in the gossipy records, there never lived a bigger liar than Rousseau. And if I personally out of long association know anything of a number of writers who are in the habit of undressing their beliefs in public, you have my word for it that the ghost of Rousseau still walks.

While I do not desire to appear in the light of an exceptional truth-teller and while frankly confessing that I entertain certain beliefs that a delicacy inherited from an illegitimate great-uncle, together with a skepticism as to the police, forbids me indiscriminately to merchant, there are certain convictions, deeply imbued in me after forty-odd years on this earth, that seem to me legitimately communicable. The first of these is that, of all philosophies governing life and conduct, that sponsored by the Cyrenaic academy, somewhat qualified, is the only one that is eminently satisfactory, eminently workable and productive of any real happiness. In a hedonism that combines the forthrightly egoistic with a modest measure of the altruistic, that governs its pleasures partly by intellect and partly by emotion — depending upon the vagaries and humors of the occasion — and that foams effervescently in the wake of work seriously and painstakingly done, I believe above all other beliefs. To me, pleasure and my own personal happiness — only infrequently collaborating with that of others — are all I deem worth a hoot. It would make me out a much finer and nobler person, I duly appreciate, to say that the happiness and welfare of all mankind were close to my heart, that nothing gave me more soulful happiness than to make others happy and that I would gladly sacrifice every cent I have in the world, together with maybe a leg, to bring a little joy to the impoverished and impaired survivors of the late Afridi raids in India, but I have difficulty in being a hypocrite. As a matter of fact, the happiness and welfare of mankind are not my profession; I am perfectly willing to leave them to the care of the professional missionaries of one sort or another; I have all that I can do to look out for my own happiness and welfare. And so has any other man, unless he happens to be a multi-millionaire, a failure in life who seeks to conceal his failure from himself in devoting himself to worse failures than himself, a gourmand of publicity, or a devout server of God. I happen to be exactly none of these — though, so far as the second catalogue goes, I surely do not view myself as a stunning success — and consequently regard myself as a sufficient problem without looking about me for other problems.

That I am selfish and to a very considerable degree possibly offensive is thus more or less regrettably obvious. All that I am able to offer in extenuation is that so are most other men if you dig down into them and, paying no attention to their altruistic pretensions, get at the hearts of them. In all my experience I have yet to find and know intimately a man worth his salt in any direction who did not think of himself first and foremost. He may drop a quarter into the hat of a beggar (when somebody is looking); he may have gracious manners; he may obey the punctilio on every occasion; he may be genial and liberal and hearty; he may buy the drinks when it comes his turn; he may be scrupulously polite, considerate and superficially lovable. But under it all his first interest, his first consideration and his first admiration are reserved for himself. The man who thinks of others before he thinks of himself may become a Grand Master of the Elks, a Socialist of parts or the star guest of honor at public banquets, but he will never become a great or successful artist, statesman or even clergyman.

Happiness is the goal of every normal human being. As it is given to few men to die happy, the best that

man can hope and strive and pray for is momentary
happiness during life, repeated as frequently as the
cards allow. Pleasure, whatever its species, is the
drink in the desert. It is the beautiful, transient reward
of travail and pain. There is no other reward, except
for those still sufficiently aboriginal to believe in an
hereafter. The ambrosia of the gods, the lovely angels,
eternal blue skies and peace, the music of golden
harps are too far off and dubious so far as my own
metaphysic goes. I prefer to trust to the more realistic
and visible Vouvray Perlier, pretty girls, Mediter-
ranean coast and symphony orchestras of the here
and now.

What makes for pleasure and consequent happiness? Each man to his own poison. In my case, a life
devoted, both professionally and in leisure hours, to
literature, drama, criticism, music and the arts generally, with due and careful heed paid to a moderate
but satisfying alcoholic diet, guaranteed by a constantly replenished wine cellar that has complacently
decided never to hear of the Eighteenth Amendment,
to decently prepared foods, to the society of selfish
and hence interesting comrades, to the amiable company of amiable women, and to the avoidance of any
and everything that might disturb my annoying equa-
nimity. The life of a writer has always seemed to me
to be about as good a one as any low human being
could hope for. His office is in his hat; his tools are in

his pocket; his boss is himself; he is foot-loose, free, clockless, independent. He can say what he wants to, however inexpedient, injudicious and discommodious, and get paid handsomely for what other working men would promptly get sacked for. He can keep his mind alive and kicking with controversy and enjoy himself in putting his inferiors in their places. He can, with relatively little work and with easy hours — if he has any talent at all — earn a very satisfactory livelihood. He moves in a world not of trade but of ideas. He deals in words, for which he doesn't have to lay out a cent and hence takes no financial risk, instead of in commodities that have to be paid for first out of his own funds. He is rewarded for his fun, like most artists, where other men are rewarded more often only for their misery. Serious or gay, he is a playboy in a world that other men run for him with the sweat of their brows.

As a very humble and lowly member of the craft and as one who still has a very considerable distance to go before he may deserve the name of artist, I can yet appreciate the tremendous advantages over other men that a real artist enjoys. In the first place, he has contempt, that most valuable of human self-wrought and self-sustained gifts. In the second place, he has liberty, freedom and autonomy — more than any other man. In the third place, he can be himself at all times and in all places. He can work when he

feels like working, loaf when he feels like loafing, keep
superiorly aloof from politics and all other such
scurvy diversions of the rabble. He is free always to
choose his friends as he will, without the usual man's
often necessary regard for their business connections
and influence; he may be indiscreet without damage
to his work; he can tell the world to go to hell and
make the world like it. If any man stands a chance
for happiness on this earth, it is the artist who has
the choicest position at the post.

Although I myself, due doubtless to defective skill,
have to work pretty hard, I do not believe in too
hard work. The hardest workers are and properly
should be the congenital clerks, book-keepers, mill-
hands and such-like pathetic incompetents and slaves.
The superior man should be able and privileged to
take life with relative ease. A life spent in constant
labor is a life wasted, save a man be such a fool as to
regard a fulsome obituary notice as ample reward.
Show me a man who, as the phrase goes, works himself
to death and I'll show you an unimaginative dolt. There
is a lot of amusement in this world and a man should
get his full share of it. There probably never lived bu
two men who gained importance and honorable celeb
rity in this selfsame world who did not take conside
able time off in which to have some sport, and of t
two exceptions one is suspect because of his peculi
taste for communion with birds, while the other fi

at least part of his story still scouted by many millions of people. Alexander the Great, even in the midst of wars, had an eye for the more comely Theban maidens; the whoopee of Caesar and Marc is history; Shakespeare spent as much time with the bottle as with the pen; Frederick and later Bismarck obeyed that impulse on many an occasion; a number of the greatest composers led the lives of movie actors; even the great Warren Gamaliel is reputed to have devoted not all of his time to affairs of state. . . .

"Work," airily observed a character in a play of the late Haddon Chambers', "is for workmen." An Englishman, Chambers once remarked to me that he had written the line as an evangelical text for Americans. I believe about work as I believe about drink: it should be used in moderation.

I believe in a college training but not in a college education. The latter, I have learned from personal experience, is worth very little; the former, which imparts a knowledge of the value and uses of leisure, a somewhat superior ease and serenity, and a humorous view of indignation, whatever form the latter may take, is not without its advantages.

I believe in the state of bachelorhood, at the very least up to the age of fifty. Thereafter, a man may conceivably marry to his benefit, but certainly not before. The arguments in favor of earlier marriage, customarily advanced by the presumptively purer of

the species, strike me as being peculiarly obscene and, where they are not obscene, hollow. The superior biological and hence inferentially superior amatory qualifications of the younger in years constitute one of the chief of these arguments. While fully conscious of the importance of sex in any contentful marital relationship, such a *plaidoyer* seems to me to be as illogical as it is indelicate, since it contends that two persons possibly ill-suited to each other in every other way — spiritually, intellectually, socially and economically — are to be recommended, endorsed and applauded as life-long companions simply on the ground of their virtuosity in anatomical arithmetic. Another favorite contention is that a man should marry while he is still malleable, that is, before he becomes set in his habits, — in other words, that the moulding of a man's character, his psyche and his future should be entrusted not to himself but to a woman. Up to the age of fifty, a man should be responsible to himself and to his work alone. A wife, however sympathetic, patient and charming, by very reason of her sympathy, patience and charm, would be a too pleasant and agreeable distraction. At fifty, a man has learned himself more or less completely, and has sounded out fully the possibilities and potentialities of his profession and his career. Then and only then should he consider matrimony. It is a rare marriage, negotiated at or after that age, that does not turn out prosperously and satisfactorily. The great majority of marriages that go on the rocks are those contracted in earlier years.

I am against all reforms and all reformers. The world, as I see it, is sufficiently gay, beautiful and happy as it stands. It is defective only to those who are themselves defective, who lack the sagacity, imagination, humor and wit to squeeze out its rich and jocose juices and go swimming in them. With Norman Douglas I agree: "I am not the stuff of which reformers are made; rather than indulge in that variety of meddlesomeness I would sweep a crossing. Nine-tenths of the reformers of humanity have been mischief-makers or humbugs. I have no desire to be added to the list. A man who has reformed himself has contributed his full share towards the reformation of his neighbor."

While I do not care for money and own to the somewhat vainglorious boast of never having consciously written a line with any thought of its marketability in mind, I am neither poseur nor fool enough to affect an air of disdain of it. The man with money in his pocket not only enjoys a power that men without money do not; he is also in a position to do his work in the world more carefully, more independently, more truthfully and more successfully. The best artists living today, the men who are doing their finest work, are without exception men who have no need longer to worry about financial matters. They have looked out for that first. A destitute and miserable man may write a good book, or paint a good picture or write a good piece of music, but the records hint that he seldom, in these days, contrives to do another.

It seems to me that the writers who are loudest in proclaiming their veneration of truth are most often simply vociferous admirers of their own pet fallacies. As for me, while given to an equal esteem of truth, I freely confess that I do not know what the truth, the final truth, about most things is and — like my colleagues alluded to — conceal my doubts and misgivings in self-persuading and, I hope, occasionally more publicly convincing convolutions of the English language, periodically enriched with more or less showy borrowings from French, German, Italian and Polack. As with most men, I believe most positively in my own ideas, right or wrong. These, to me, constitute the truth, whatever others may think of them. Once I believe a thing head and tail, no one can alter my conviction.

It also seems to me that the current fashionable American literary school of cynicism as to sentiment, love and romance is cheapjack, fraudulent and silly. The American, as I have on more than one occasion observed, being generically the most sentimental of men, is ashamed of his sentiment and, like a man with thinning hair who drops miscellaneous jokes at the expense of baldheads, seeks to conceal or at least to divert uncomfortable attention from the fact by deprecating it in others. The most cynical writers in America today are personally so many honeydew melons, happily and sweetly sentimental husbands and fathers. It is merely that, like uncertain and unconfident men ever, they offer their public protestations of hard-boiled manliness — in the American definition — in order to hide from their womenfolk, laughing up their sleeves, their irresolution, nervousness, weakness and innate childishness. Romantic love is the privilege of emperors, kings, soldiers and artists; it is the butt of democrats, traveling salesmen, magazine poets and the writers of American novels.

My code of life and conduct is simply this: work hard, play to the allowable limit, disregard equally the good or bad opinion of others, never do a friend a dirty trick, eat and drink what you feel like when you feel like, never grow indignant over anything, trust to tobacco for calm and serenity, bathe twice a day, modify the aesthetic philosophy of Croce but slightly with that of Santayana and achieve for one's self a pragmatic sufficiency in the beauty of the aesthetic surface of life, learn to play at least one musical instrument and then play it only in private, never allow one's self even a passing thought of death, never contradict anyone or seek to prove anything to anyone unless one gets paid for it in cold, hard coin, live the moment to the utmost of its possibilities, treat one's enemies with polite inconsideration, avoid persons who are chronically in need, and be satisfied with life always but never with one's self. An infinite belief in the possibilities of one's self with a coincidental critical assessment and derogation of one's achievements, self-respect combined with a measure of self-surgery, aristocracy of mind combined with democracy of heart, forthrightness with modesty or at least with good manners, dignity with a quiet laugh, honor and honesty and decency: these are the greatest qualities that man can hope to attain. And as one man, my hope is to attain them.

I am against snobbery in all its lovely American forms. As a born American, I suppose that I am naturally and unpleasantly infected with some of the bacteria, but I keep about me constantly a large and handy assortment of antitoxins. I am for all religions equally, as all impress me as being equally hollow. The variation is merely one either of external and superficial beauty or hideousness of spectacle. I believe that no man's life is finally complete and rounded — to quote an eminent Hungarian — without a wife, a child, a home, though I have not practiced what I preach and have neither wife nor child and live in that apologetic substitute for a home, a New York apartment. (It looks out on a building given over to shyster lawyers!) I believe, with Nietzsche, though I dislike the banality of dragging him forth on every occasion, that so long as you are praised, believe that you are not yet on your own course but on that of another. And also that it happens sometimes by an exception that a man only reaches the highest when he disclaims his ideal, for this ideal previously drove him onward too violently, so that in the middle of the track he regularly got out of breath and had to rest.

I respect J. Pierpont Morgan but not Rockefeller. Morgan is hard-fisted, hard-punching, ruthless, brave, forthrightly avaricious and lacking in all hypocrisy. Rockefeller, a moral coward, wraps himself in the seven veils of church and charity by way of concealing the true golden-yellow color of his psychical epidermis from the public eye. I admire Clemenceau for his courageous errors and disrelish Wilson for his cowardly exactitudes. I have no patriotism, for patriotism, as I see it, is often an arbitrary veneration of real estate above principles. I believe that one intelligent man is worth ten parcel of beautiful women, but I would rather spend an evening with the beautiful women. I believe that intelligent men should be taken on at lunch. I believe that whiskey and gin are bad for the system and that wine and beer are more beneficial to it than all the drugstore philtres in Christendom. I owe my glowing health to wines and beers,

although I occasionally drink whiskey and gin and
find that, despite my belief to the contrary, they do
not seem to do any particular damage. I believe that
Richard Strauss is the only substantial living com-
poser, that Sinclair Lewis is the most significant American novelist, though Willa Cather is the best writer,
that there is not a living statesman worth serious consideration, that Stephen Phillips is a much greater
poet than many think, that the only young serious
dramatist in Europe worth talking about is Franz
Werfel, that one of the sharpest humorists that America has produced is W. E. Hill, that the most beautiful
spot in the world is a certain little inn hidden away
on the bank of a stream in the Black Forest, that
Lindbergh, Coste, Byrd and all that crew are absurd
futilitarians, that the best place to eat on earth is, first,
Madame Génot's in the Rue de la Banque, Paris, and,
second, the Vieux Logis in the Rue Lepic of the same
town, that Spatenbräu is the most perfect beer, that
the faint cinnamon smell of a carnation is the most
gratifying of all flower perfumes, that the only completely original playwright since Ibsen is Pirandello,
that the only authentic gentlemen left in the world are
the Austrians, that athletic sports, save in the case of
young boys, are designed for idiots, that money is
meant to be spent and not saved, that since we are all
now duly and perfectly aware that America has its
full share of Rotarians, Kiwanians and Ku Kluxers,

not to mention the Anti-Saloon League, the W. C. T. U., the Y. M. C. A., the D. A. R. and the Methodist Board of Temperance, Prohibition and Public Morals, we may as well stop harping on the subject, that it is occasionally well, by way of making the world more palatable, to indulge one's self luxuriously in a remission of judgment and delude one's self momentarily with illusion, and that, when all is said and done, each and every man's philosophy of life, whatever it may be, is profoundly right so long as it makes him happy.

# BOOK II: PROVERBS

## § 1

*The Destructive Critic.*— There never lived a so-called destructive critic who, if his destructive criticism had not been eminently sound, would not have passed into oblivion in very short order. A critic, whatever the designation applied to him, lives by the grace, interest and intelligence of his readers. To argue, therefore, that this or that critic is purely destructive is to imply that all his reading adherents are also of purely destructive tendencies. And nothing could be sillier.

## § 2

*Creative Writing.*— Of all the definitions mouthed by a certain branch of the critical fraternity, that which has to do with creation in literary fields is the most completely bogus. It is the persistent theory of the branch in point that the phrase *creative writing* must be reserved for novelists, poets and writers of a kind, however bad, and that it cannot truthfully be visited upon any others, however good. Criticism, according to the definition, does not come under the head of creation and, as a consequence, such things as Dryden's "Essay of Dramatic Poesy" are not creative writing whereas such things as Zane Grey's novels presumably are. Nor does journalism in any form meet with the favor of the definition, with the result that the late Richard Harding Davis' description of the entrance of the German troops into Belgium is consigned to limbo, whereas the same writer's worst short fiction gains the good graces of the definition. The whole business, like so much of critical theory, is the purest nonsense. Frank Harris' journalism has often been creative writing of a high order. So has Shaw's and Wells'. What, too, of Addison's, Steele's, Swift's and Lamb's? And as for critical creative writing, what of Philip Sidney's, Corneille's, Samuel Johnson's, Lessing's, Voltaire's, Schiller's and Zola's?

## § 3

*The Thinking Pen.*— Another of the fallacies that hovers over the literary art is that the writer who thinks clearly will pretty generally write clearly, whereas the one whose thought is muddled will write in a muddled manner. The late Conan Doyle, when he entered the field of spooks and metaphysics, showed a mind as muddled as a tureen of provincial soup, yet he wrote simply, clearly and, so far as mere

writing goes, effectively. The same is presently true
of Chesterton when he goes in for religion, as it is
true of Croce when he tackles the higher metaphysics
of criticism. On the other hand, a measure of the
writing of the world's foremost and clearest philosophical thinkers is, from the viewpoint of mere
writing as writing, ambiguous, defective, involved
and clumsy. For one Nietzsche or Huxley who has
written as lucidly as he thought, you will find sufficient instances of clear thought transcribed groggily
to paper — by way of example, some portions of
Spinoza's "Ethics" and many more in the works of
Kant.

The fallacy of the short sentence as a symbol of
clear and direct thought is equally persistent. The
clearest and most important philosophical thought
that has been contributed to man has often been expressed in sentences so long that it is difficult to remember the beginning of them by the time one has
plowed one's way past the middle. The most planless
and idiotic thought of the most idiotic writers has
been visited upon us in the crisp, short and speciously
effective sentences of political diatribes, newspaper
editorials and dime novels.

§ 4

*The Counterpoint of Detraction.*— Just as an otherwise taciturn person is seized peculiarly with an impulse to talk the moment a doctor sticks a clinical thermometer into his mouth, so is even the most linguacious critic rendered peculiarly mute when confronted by an indubitably fine piece of work. The latter, once the prefatory hallelujahs are done with, leaves so little for him to say; the artist has said that say so much better than he can say it in his rôle of mere liaison echo. This is why we often find critics, even the best of them, driven to the resort of praising meritorious work in terms of detraction of certain other more or less related work. The counterpoint of detraction gives them the necessary ground to dig their heels into; it vouchsafes them an articulateness that would otherwise be difficult.

§ 5

*Personal Chemistry.*— Scrutinizing the body of critical practice in America, one wen in particular takes on a painful conspicuity. The outstanding flaw in this critical body is not, as is often maintained by critics of criticism, a cheap level of artistic judgment, but rather a cheap level of personal chemistry. Among our critics we have men whose opinions are honest, sound and convincing, but we also have many more whose opinions, while perhaps equally honest and sound so far as they go, lack complete conviction because of an infiltration, which they cannot conceal, of the essentially snide men they themselves are. A snide man may write intelligent criticism, but he cannot write criticism that persuades others save intelligent men who are similarly snide. Out of some of the most interesting criticism being written in America today there steam traces of this snideness, and the impression that one consequently gets of it is of a deodorant applied not so much to the art and persons it criticizes as to the authentic, half-sensed and sweatingly concealed shabbiness of the critic himself.

§ 6

*Reply to Criticism.*— To a very considerable extent, the prevalence and persistence of so much half-baked and factitious criticism are due, I believe, to the unwritten law that obtains among first-rate artists regarding the answering of criticism of themselves, however asinine and contemptible that criticism may be. It is held by such artists to be beneath dignity to reply to criticism of any kind, whether laudatory or deprecatory, and they generally stick to the principle of an aloof and even snooty silence. There has, indeed, come to be something suspect about the artist who condescends to reply to criticism of himself; his fellows view him down a superior nose; and, appreciating this, it is a rare craftsman found willing to lower himself by meeting honey with acid or — more important — brick with brick. As a consequence, the worst sort of critical grease or insult, cheap back-slapping or cheap rear-booting, is permitted to go unnoticed and unchallenged, and ignorant criticism is allowed to flourish in the land and wax fat on its ignorance.

The tradition that a first-rate man is less a first-rate man if, encountering a cheap detraction of himself that has no respect for the facts, he makes critical riposte, strikes me as being just about as grotesque as anything I have run across during many years spent in this grotesque world. I speak, of course and obviously enough, not of cheap criticism written by essentially cheap men, but of the species of cheap criticism that is every once in a while written by men who should know better. When a jackass brays, no one pays any attention to him, not even other jackasses. But when a lion brays like a jackass, even the lions in the neighborhood may be pardoned for exhibiting a little surprise and for looking around to observe what has befallen their brother. It is this kind of braying, sometimes issuing from lions and more often from sheep and jackals in lions' clothing, that chronically disturbs the critical air in the American jungle, and that disturbs the peace of its artists. A few well-placed shots, with the necessary ammunition fully at the artists' command, would do a lot to dimin-

ish the racket and bring some semblance of critical
dignity back to the landscape. If the authentic artists
amongst us continue to be insulted by so much shabby,
disreputable, dishonest and offensive criticism, it will
be their fault and theirs alone. Let there be an end
to this hypocritical posturing and let a first-rate man,
when he is trifled with by fifth-rate criticism, hit back.
The greatest artists of the past have not hesitated to
answer their ignorant critics with the gunpowder of
their sounder intelligence. The artists that we have
today are simply affected mountebanks if they hesitate to do the same thing.

§ 7

*Pedestal Pullers.*— One of the things one never
fails to notice in American criticism is the apparent
glee with which the bulk of that criticism hops upon
defective work on the part of an established American
artist. It seems that the average American critic lies
eagerly in wait for an artist not to do as good work as
he has previously done or better, but for him to produce something inferior. And when he does, the critic
betrays clearly his air of rejoicing. Dreiser, Cabell,
Anderson, Lewis, O'Neill and other such men, falling
now and then for the moment below the standards they
have imposed upon themselves, have thus found themselves treated like knaves and imposters. Where the

European critic always wishes for the best in his artists, the American critic gives one the feeling that he is always hoping for the worst. We have no plainer symptom than this of the fundamental self-uncertainty and priggishness of American criticism and of its vain desire to raise itself to a position of relative eminence by increasing the number of corpses to stand upon.

§ 8

*Critical Dodge.*— In much the same category as our young so-called radical playwrights who attempt to conceal the fact that they have nothing to say by saying it in a new and alarming manner, fall certain of our critics who, also having nothing new to say, attempt to conceal the fact by saying it in that quiet, précieuse, old-fashioned manner that passes in certain quarters for dignity of mind and solidity of judgment.

§ 9

*Critical Disparagement.*— The kind of criticism that is ladled out to our more mature artists must often reduce them to a rueful laughter. Lewis, when he writes an "Elmer Gantry," is met with the objection that — I quote literally from no less than thirty reviewers —"the book contains scarcely a decent character; almost all of them are hypocrites, scoundrels and vile." The same criticism may be made of Gorki's admitted masterpiece, "Nachtasyl." Dreiser, when he writes a novel twice as long as one of, say, Christopher Morley's, is charged with the very embonpoint and dispansion for which Dostoievski is acclaimed. Cabell is disparaged for doing what the Restoration writers are commended for. Sherwood Anderson is criticized for faults that in Zola are held to be virtues. And O'Neill is made mock of, in his finest play, for daring a profound and beautiful thing, far removed from the routine swamps of Broadway, instead of safely hugging the critical coasts with more of his youthful confections wherein a supposed spy's secret documents turn out to be love letters, wherein a Swede is given knock-out drops in a gin-mill, and wherein everybody goes crazy in a green light looking for gold or ile.

§ 10

*Prejudice.*— It is unreasonable to ask of me that I approach each and every book or play with an open and unprejudiced mind. That is to be expected only of the critical amateur and dilettante. Behind every book or play there is an author or a playwright and behind the author or playwright there is, in many instances, a record of previous performance. Where a complete lack of merit has been observable in such antecedent performances, I find myself unable to approach the new work without a certain prejudice against it. This prejudice has not turned out to be ill-founded, I have discovered, for in a quarter of a century of reviewing I have never known a case where an author or a playwright already put down as talentless has suddenly and miraculously turned into a genius overnight. The possibility that he may produce something worthwhile is an argument of critical commentators who, were they race-track followers, would be of the kind who, fondly hoping against hope, would regularly and to their ultimate woe play 200 to 1 shots. If, as might by a wild flight of fancy happen, one such incompetent were actually one day to write a really good book or play, I should be only too glad to change my point of view and confess to my prejudicial error. But until that day comes, I shall continue to cherish my advance conviction that this or that author or playwright will present me with nothing that is worth my serious consideration and thought.

§ 11

*Critic Versus Critic.*— The healthiest promise of American criticism is the increasing criticism of criticism, observable in many quarters. Twenty years ago, critics seldom, if ever, criticized one another and the

result was largely an enthronement of critical nonsense
and a general critical stagnation. I myself, criticizing
the prevailing critics of that day, was considered a
very impolite fellow and was regarded in the light
of a violator of the punctilio. Today, all is changed —
and for the better. Every critic is open to attack by all
other critics. The bricks fly back and forth and the
soft-heads are knocked out to the improvement of the
critical art, literature and drama. If our criticism,
literature and drama have advanced, it has been these
bricks that have been largely responsible.

§ 12

*Advance of Literary Criticism.*—Contemporary literary criticism in America has advanced out of all
proportion to contemporary dramatic criticism for the
simple reason that the materials being provided to
the former are infinitely more inspiring and provoca-
tive than those being provided to the latter. Accurate,
intelligent and even shrewdly humorous criticism of
negligible drama remains, after a while, static; there
is no soil in which it may develop and grow. This,
I appreciate, is a platitude but this, it seems to me,
is the time to repeat it. It is easy to interest and amuse
readers with criticism of contemptible drama, provided one be sufficiently skilful with the pen, but
contemptible drama is the greatest foe of criticism

itself. Behind every great dramatic critic you will find one or more great dramatists.

## § 13

*Exit Indignation.*— The greatest virtue of the United States in a cultural direction lies in its gradual diminution of one's primitive impulse to indignation. The truly cultured man is never indignant, and toward that civilized desideratum the country operates in a proficient manner. It is impossible for a man to live in the United States for long and still be indignant over its laws, acts, invasions of right, lack of honor, hypocrisy, sordidness and vindictiveness. Of these there is such a surplusage, constantly on the increase, that the indignation initially engendered gradually becomes worn out under the strain and is transmuted into either a sardonic humor or a mood of *laissez-faire*. The American over thirty-five or forty who can still work himself up to a red face over the indignities, chicaneries and hypocrisies practiced so generally in the nation is invariably an American of the lower and negligible human order. The more civilized American can only, after his long acquaintanceship with the state of affairs, sadly blow his nose and let out a derisory groan. After a man has fought in the trenches for many verminous years, his indignation is much less against the enemy than against his own command-

ing officers and the principles and the country that
they serve.

§ 14

*Honesty of Opinion.*— Honesty of opinion is not
unusual in American critical writing. The weakness of
much of that writing lies in its failure to combine the
honesty of opinion with basically sound judgment.

§ 15

*Journalistic Dramatic Criticism.*— Paradoxical as
it may superficially seem, the considerable improvement in the standards of American journalistic dramatic criticism, widely observable, is doubtless responsible for the alienation from the theatre of many
hitherto regular playgoers. Up to as recently as ten
or twelve years ago, general newspaper theatrical
reviewing was largely indistinguishable from the paid
theatrical advertising on the same page. Its apparent
purpose was to endorse almost everything indiscriminately, irrespective of its merits, to remain in the
warm graces of managers, producers, playwrights and
even actors, and to cotton to the old newspaper policy
of saying something nice about all possible big adver-
tisers and taking a chance in the other direction with
everyone else except Catholic clergymen and Jewish
bankers. The notion that this constant ballyhooing of

inferior theatrical goods drove people in disgust from
the theatre — a theory advanced by sundry professors
of the drama in the literary reviews — is hardly borne
out by the facts. For the facts are that the theatre in
the period under discussion was enormously prosperous and that, in the period that directly followed, it
took the public so long to get over the salubrious effects
of the ballyhooing that it was more prosperous still.

The newspaper reading public, which is the potential theatregoing public, wants and craves good notices
of plays, however lack-brained, and is disgruntled
when it does not get them. It wants news, however un-
founded, of plays to go to, not plays to stay away
from. It reads the papers to find out what to do with
its evenings, not to find out what not to do. And the
latter is what, under the recent more intelligent and
more honest critical dispensation, it pretty generally
finds. Thus, as theatrical reviewing, with the newspapers' concurrence, has become more forthright, fair
and above-board, it has more and more discouraged
theatregoing as a public diversion. It is all very well
to argue that bad plays still succeed and draw in the
crowds despite bad notices, but for one that does so
you will find twenty or thirty that do not, and the
theatre as an institution is surely helped no more by
that brand of success than by such failures. The public, or at least a sufficiently paying share of it, likes
bad plays and good notices of them give it the neces-

sary stimulus, encouragement and self-substantiation
to go to them and thereafter gabble enthusiastically
about the fine time that was had.

The standard of theatrical reviewing in the daily
papers has become altogether too high for the public,
and the public is being frightened away from the
theatre as a consequence. Men of some taste and training and probity have taken the place of such lardy
fellows of the past as Alan Dale, Acton Davies and
company, and, instead of the old whooping up of
plays right and left, the public is now getting the low-
down. It isn't ready for the low-down; it doesn't relish
it; and it is scared. What it needs, wants and doubtless
again longs for are not the present eulogies of Chekhov's oblique dramaturgy and denunciations of Mr.
Myron C. Fagan's somewhat more direct, but the old-
time enthusiastic tributes to the genius of neo-Charles
Kleins, the beauty of neo-Maxine Elliotts and the
great thrills of neo-"Way Down Easts." To believe
that the public wants no such thing is to believe that
a public that is a gull in every other direction suddenly and miraculously constitutes itself a compen-
dium of wisdom in the presence of the theatre.

§ 16

*Purity of Speech.*— Clear speech in the theatre is
all very well, but it may be carried too far. The critics

have much to answer for in this regard. They have harped upon perfect enunciation so insistently that they have frightened the poor actors to death. The result is often a comical distortion of dramatic values, with actors playing gutter tramps reading their lines with the painstaking precision of professors of English and with others playing hayseeds laboriously manoeuvering their wads of American chewing tobacco out of the way of the King's tongue.

## § 17

*The Humanists.*— It seems to me that the critics of the Humanists have overlooked the one elemental point that, more than all other points combined, has directly motivated their late activity. Through the smoke-screen that they have adroitly thrown around themselves, this point remains as clear as day. The prose elephantiasis which gives their logic a bogus aspect of size, the hokum of an arbitrary and well-timed opposition to the current critical predilection, the air of authority which always attaches to a championship of the traditions, however empty, the college degrees strung after the names of many of them — these have served to obscure in impressionable minds what is really back of the whole business. And, though an imputation of personal motives is not always in the nicest critical taste, I violate the critical punctilio to the extent of hazarding what is undoubtedly the main-spring of the whole Humanist movement as it presently reveals itself.

That main-spring, unless I am sadly in error, is a personal envy, long concealed but with concealment obviously no longer possible to the Humanists, of the critics who now for more than fifteen years have dictated American tastes, have gained fame and fortune in the dictating, and have in the process had a devil of a good time. These critics have thrust the espousers of Humanism so far into the background that the latter have been hardly discernible; they have for years been cruelly neglected by editors; their checks from magazines and newspaper literary supplements have been conspicuous for their absence; their books have not sold; they have been buried, to their disappointment and agony, under the saleable and remunerative doctrines marketed by their opponents. These opponents, some of them not very profound but all of them forceful, persuasive and exciting writers and showmen, have been sitting pretty, as the vernacular has it, for so long that it has got on the Humanists' nerves. And what has irritated the latter more — for such is the deplorable way of human nature — are the gay, happy and carefree personalities and lives of the men who for years have been enjoying their profitable day in the critical court.

The Humanists, most of them poorly paid college

professors and even more poorly paid assistant professors and instructors, to say nothing of contributors — by force of circumstances and necessity — to the one and two cents-a-word periodicals, are personally disappointed, defeated, discontented and unhappy fellows. The joy and gaiety of life have been denied them; their audiences of college boys have slowly fossilized them; their confinement in outhouses of education has embittered them, not as teachers but as men. And all the while they have looked out into the world and seen the gay circus parade of criticism, wrapped in confetti, singing down the highways. They stood it for as long as they could, but found that they could stand it no longer. And so, after their kind and unable to do anything else about it, they called in the metaphorical police.

It is not the doctrines and methods of the antithetical school of criticism that the new Humanists oppose so much as it is the advocates and practitioners of those doctrines and methods personally. That is, as men. And, as Lewis Mumford has so aptly put it, their strength, as with a Chinese army, consists largely in their war-cries and their dreadful faces. They are not so much against the critical professions of their enemies as against the disturbing fact that the latter have been riding on the crest of the wave and have been splashing around in grand glee. For these others are, as has been hinted, by nature and in mode of living, gleeful fellows. They drink good liquor; they like to wink at pretty girls; they have money in their pockets; they like to play and sing; they are cocky, as all successful and happy men are cocky; they don't give a damn. And that is what makes the dry, bitter and disillusioned other side mad. It thinks of Huneker with a love letter from Mary Garden in his pants-pocket, a great *Seidel* of Pilsner before him, and a feather in his pearl-gray Fedora. It thinks of Mencken, his shirt off, playing Wiener waltzes on a piano, the while a Baltimore coon stands close by with a magnum of Niersteiner, and it thinks of Mencken's large holdings of real estate along the lovely Chesapeake and the two blondes who once chased him half a mile up the boulevards in Paris. It thinks of O'Neill in his magnificent chateau in the Loire country, of Dreiser revelling in his estates up the Hudson, of Harry Elmer Barnes hobnobbing with the Kaiser at Doorn and sucking up the old boy's choicest *Schnapps*, of Tom Beer's Rolls-Royce and of Sinclair Lewis' $130,000 annual income. It thinks of Lewis Mumford being courted by half the editors in the country, of Cabell retired to his Virginia estates at the early age of fifty, of Lewisohn at ease in France, his books selling to the tune of 80,000, of Waldo Frank being met at South American steamship docks by bands and dusky beauties, of Spingarn lolling in his great house up the Hudson and lazily bestirring himself only to fetch up another bottle from the cellar and coincidentally to dismiss Humanism in a small three-page folder. It thinks of the late Percy Pollard, who led the life of a country gentleman, and of the late Vance Thompson, who had a grand time in the embassy at Rome, and of the late Bill Reedy, whose middle got to be so contentedly and beautifully ample that they had to move the beer-table up to *him*. It thinks of Carl Van Doren, at the head of a great book business, of Henry Seidel Canby — no longer condemned merely to the instruction of college boys — also at the head of one and the editor of a fast-growing literary weekly to boot, of Walter Lippmann who came within an ace of getting Peggy Joyce's elaborate town house for himself, of Van Wyck Brooks sufficiently well-heeled to be able to take life easy, of Joseph Wood Krutch profiting from soft magazine posts and big book sales. It thinks of these and of many others like them, and it becomes good and indignant.

For what do we see as the other side of the picture? We see Irving Babbitt condemned to end his days — he is already sixty-six — lecturing his head off to college striplings, and Paul Elmer More, already sixty-seven, buried haplessly in a little New Jersey college town, a sad old man. We see young Seward Collins, his money in the *Bookman*, struggling pathetically against the big circulations of the magazines of his hated rivals. We see young Gorham B. Munson des-

perately ekeing out a livelihood talking to women's
clubs and jitney forums. We see Norman Foerster,
the best of the younger lot, condemned to tutoring in
a North Carolina factory of learning. We see Christian
Gauss at fifty-one still wielding the birch over college
youngsters, and Robert Shafer despairing in a school
in Cincinnati, Ohio. And we see a lot of others of the
same kind in similar dismal holes.

Is it, therefore, I ask you in all politeness, any
wonder?

§ 18

*America and the Artist.*— The lamentation, so
often ventilated by incompetent and disgruntled
craftsmen, that the United States treats its artists
badly — if, indeed, it even so much as gives them a
passing thought — is hardly borne out by the noticeable affluence of most of them, by the exaggerated
amount of attention they get from the public press
and by the abundance of invitations they receive to
lend their not always too *soigné* presences to dinners,
banquets, ladies' club teas, movie openings, lecture
platforms, blindfold tests of cigarettes, dedicatory
exercises, and booze parties on the ocean liners. I have
grave doubts that in any other country in the world
is a meritorious artist so rewarded and petted as he
is in this one. And I entertain even graver doubts that
he wouldn't be much better off if well-intentioned

dolts would leave him alone, allow him to keep his
mind solely on his work, and so permit him to function in peace and quiet to his greater glory. The United
States not only does not disdain its artists; it goes to
the extreme of coddling them so greatly, both in the
way of personal attention and financial reward, that it
often damn nigh ruins them.

The trouble with the lamenters, even those few who
have a share of sense, is that they allege against the
country as a whole an inattention and lack of sympathy that one actually finds mainly in a single quarter, and that quarter a high one. The American artist's
chief neglect is not at the hands of what may be called
the average American, but at the hands of Americans of
wealth, Americans conspicuous in public affairs,
Americans of position in what is dubbed society and
Americans who might be presumed, however erron-
eously, to have some breeding, discrimination and
taste. It is this class, which in another nation often
offers a warming hospitality and cordiality to the
artist, that here is hostile and apathetic to him or, if
not exactly hostile and apathetic, that regards him
with a sniffish casualness and unconcern. With the
single exception of the late Henry H. Rogers — and,
possibly, John Quinn — I can think of no rich American who during his lifetime has ever intelligently be-
friended a worthy American artist. The Maecenases
of the present day decline to endorse deserving artists

and prefer to visit their patronage instead upon jazz bands, combustible young operatic sopranos, alley-theatre playwrights, English novelists with pretty parlor manners, and leg shows.

The American artist must look for his reward from the masses of the people, not from those who might ordinarily be expected, by the standards of other countries, to take a perhaps greater and more friendly interest in him. This reward the American in the mass accords him. But this reward is almost invariably withheld from him by the American of relative eminence. The Presidents of the United States, for example, for the last twenty years, with one exception, have proudly announced themselves to be devourers of cheap detective stories. The exception, Roosevelt, caused a national consternation by announcing that he had once read a novel by Owen Johnson, and had liked it.

§ 19

*The Critic Barred.*— In the matter of indignant protestation against the exclusion of critics from theatres by managers vexed by the former's animadversions, I have never been able to bring myself to participate, for the simple reason that I can't see the sense of being indignant over the exercise of any man's inalienable rights, however much of an ass I personally may consider him. To argue that a theatrical manager hasn't a right to keep anyone he wishes to out of his theatre, provided only the objectionable person be white, is not only to tilt with the legal statutes — already tested in the courts by outraged and inflammable reviewers and found holding — but also to argue that a theatrical manager alone of all men must mutely tolerate and endure damaging onslaughts upon his business, his capital and his immortal honor.

In a quarter of a century of dramatic criticism I, like other members of the reviewing fraternity, have on occasion incurred the displeasure of certain managers and producers and have been duly informed that my critical presence in their theatres was, to put it politely, unwelcome. But on none of these occasions has it ever occurred to me to object to the gentlemen's edicts, as, after brief meditation, I have come to the conclusion that they were most often, according to their peculiar lights, perfectly justified in their decision.

Let us consider these aforementioned lights. In one case, many years ago, I was barred from a certain theatre because, in a review of one of the manager's productions, I recorded the observation that the leading actress was atrocious, giving in detail my reasons for visiting the adjective upon the lady. To the casual reader, it might seem that barring a critic for such a cause constituted the last word in hypocrisy and the first word in throttling honest critical opinion. But the casual reader would have no means of knowing, as I subsequently had, that the actress in question happened to be the manager's esoteric *chère amie*, a fact which made his attitude toward me and my critique not only understandably clear but even one to be acutely sympathized with. It certainly would be unfair to say against this particular manager that only a theatrical manager would act as he did, for the history of composers, painters and littérateurs who have made public fools of themselves on similar grounds amply attests to the truth of the old saw that human nature, say what you will, is human nature. To contend, further, that the manager in point, idiot though he seemed to me, did any serious damage to the noble art of dramatic criticism by ostracizing me, would be doubly and even triply idiotic. Just what great value I served the world of serious and important criticism by pointing out the painfulness of some poor woman's attempt at acting in a completely negligible play — neither of which was worth criticism in the first place — I'll be hanged if I know. And since the manager, in the three years that I continued to be excluded from his productions, produced plays that were unanimously denounced by my more reputable colleagues as entirely worthless, I further cannot see that my absence from his showhouses was in any way to be deplored. Certainly it was not deplored by me and I, according to these friendly colleagues, was supposed to be the injured party.

It is a curious phenomenon of the American theatre that, in its entire latter-day record, no manager or producer of what we may call artistic repute has ever been known to close his doors to criticism, however ill-advised or personally objectionable it may have been to him. If there is a single exception to this statement, I should like to have it brought to my notice. The only half-way exception that I can think of is Mr. Walter Hampden, and the only critic he has ever excluded from his performances is none other than the humble writer of these lines. Nor did even this Hampden fail to invite me to criticize his efforts until about a year and a half ago, after I had announced that long and studious observation of his work convinced me that he was simply a handsome fellow with a fine speaking voice who knew absolutely nothing of the art of acting, and had thereupon advertised that I would henceforth bar myself from further and to me wholly wasteful contemplations of his strivings. In Mr. Hampden's somewhat belated decision to exclude me from his future performances, I therefore not only fully concurred but found myself an enthusiastic collaborator. For I should certainly feel about things exactly the way he did if a literary critic said that he would no longer review any of my books on the ground that, though I was an Adonisian fellow indeed, I did not know the least thing about writing. That critic would plainly be spared the agony of any more books.

From time to time in my long reviewing career, I have followed the principle of self-exclusion that I practiced in the case of Mr. Hampden's exhibitions, and have duly chronicled the news in my reviewing columns. I have done this, in each instance, for two reasons: first and obviously, because I deemed it a sad waste of valuable time and a sad boring of my readers to go on criticizing the efforts of completely incompetent men and, secondly, because I considered it unfair to such incompetents to go on proclaiming them incompetents in the name of dignified criticism that, to deserve its name, should have absolutely nothing to do with them. Thus, after reviewing the producing efforts of Mr. Gustav Blum for a period of years and finding them beneath the notice of any critic devoted to the higher interests of drama, I automatically barred myself from any view of the gentleman's future exhibits and from any chronicle of those exhibits in print. Thus, too, I barred myself and my pen from the stages presided over by Mr. Butler Davenport, Mr. John Henry Mears, Mr. Michael Kallesser and others. I am glad to leave jests at these poor fellows' expense to such reviewers as still elect to fritter away time over their monkeyshines in the name of dramatic art. I do not wish to go on telling the same funny story over and over again. I find it difficult to laugh at the same joke continuously.

Not long ago, one of our producers telephoned to me and said: "I am putting on a play next week that will not interest you critically in the slightest; it is pretty poor stuff from any sound critical point of view and I am simply hoping to make some money out of it — I need some, as I got hit badly in the stock market crash. I've read your dramatic criticism for twenty years and I know that, according to your standards, you'd walk out on the play after the curtain had been up fifteen minutes. So I won't invite you to review the play and waste your time on it."

Now that is what I call excellent sense! I thanked the gentleman for his honesty and for his implied generosity toward my standards of criticism and assured him that if his fellow producers were as forthright and above-board with reviewers when they put on poor plays designed simply as box-office bumpers, there would be a greatly increased measure of goodwill all around. But many producers have not this one's simple rectitude. They know that the stuff they produce is utterly worthless from any valid critical point of view, but they hope against hope that the reviewers will be fooled. Well, the reviewers are not often fooled — although there are occasional exceptions which encourage the producers to go on deluding themselves — and the producers wax wrathful when the reviewers announce their wares for the rubbish they, the producers, know perfectly well they are.

Mr. Arthur Hopkins sometimes denounces the critics for views of his productions which he does not agree with, but he never excludes any one of them, however much he disagrees with him, from those productions. He believes wholeheartedly in the plays he selects and is naturally, honestly and understandably disappointed when the critics do not coincide in his opinion of the plays in point, and naturally, honestly and even understandably does not hesitate to say so in print, but he does not superiorly set himself and his own views atop a pedestal by keeping the critics in the future out of his theatre. And there are other producers like him in this respect. These are, as I have observed, generally the worthwhile men in our theatre.

But, even so, it seems to me that there are grounds on which a critic — the word in this case should be enclosed in quotation marks — may properly be barred from a theatre by a disgusted, reputable producer. Why such a producer should be expected to continue to allow any immature, artistically inexperienced and generally incompetent young man either regularly to denounce or to flatter his productions, I cannot see. The whole point about the justice or injustice of barring a critic lies in the question of the critic's capabilities. If he is generally recognized to be a capable critic, whatever his prejudices, any manager who bars him is open to the suspicion of being an artistic fraud, a vainglorious posturer, a mountebank and a cheap coward. But if the self-styled critic is simply a pretender to the critical craft and one whose passport to the theatre is simply a critical false-face, the manager who bars him is not only doing a service to himself and to the art of the theatre and drama, but is also doing a service to criticism in general. The manager, however, sometimes fails to discriminate between the two species of critics and so makes a caricature of himself.

Every intelligent man, whatever the field of his activities, has certain prejudices and it is therefore only reasonable to expect the intelligent critic to have certain prejudices along with the rest of his fellow artists. If these prejudices are born of experience, education and taste, they are, whatever you or I may think of them, the critic's right to hold and to maintain. A critic without prejudices, presuming him to be a critic of some standing, is merely a useless piece of soft soap. Prejudice is often synonymous with experience and the test which that experience has provided a critic. Against such prejudice, based upon training, culture and sound discrimination, no manager or producer is justified in taking issue at the door of his playhouse. There are always the public prints in which any such issue may be resorted to; the public prints display a considerable hospitality to both manager

and producer in this direction. But where prejudices
are based upon matters apart from drama, where they
are founded not upon a producer's, playwright's or
an actor's work but upon some thing or things dissoci-
ated from what are properly the critic's concern, then
the manager and the producer are entirely justified not
only in keeping the offending writer out of their theatres but in giving him a swift kick into the bargain.

Again, however, the trouble with certain managers
and producers is that they sometimes go out of their
ways to read personalities into criticisms that, though
they must inevitably mention names, are anything but
personal. It is a well-known fact that the first thing
that pops out of a printed page at the reader is the
mention of his own name. And the moment a manager
or producer suffers this pop he is in the habit of ex-
pecting the worst. He looks for the worst and, even
when it is not there, somehow feels that at least a trace
of it is concealed somewhere about the premises. He
craves personal mention; he will do anything to get
it; yet he is not sure of himself when he does get it.
The least derogation of his talents and he looks upon
the critic with a baleful and suspicious eye. The critic
may whack the life out of the producer's playwright,
his scene designer, his actors or anyone else, but let
him so much as register a doubt about the producer
himself and the latter's blood begins to boil. So long
as criticism is directed against others, the producer

does not often mind. But the moment it gets near his own skin, a critical eczema sets in. When you hear of a critic who has been barred by a producer or manager, accordingly, it is generally a safe wager that the barring is the result of the critic's having touched upon the producer or manager himself.

The whole business of critic-barring may be summed up thus: *1.* Any manager or producer is perfectly within his rights in barring any critic he elects to; *2.* Some so-called critics should be barred by any manager or producer who has the best interests of drama, the theatre and criticism at heart; *3.* But the exclusion of any reputable and capable critic by a manager or producer is simply a confession of that manager's or producer's own shortcomings.

## § 20

*Outcast.*— A destructive critic seems by the prevailing definition to be one who does not like bad plays that certain other persons think are good, and who says so. And not only bad plays, but bad books, bad music, bad actors and bad critics. (In Europe, of course, destructive critic is a compliment, like permitting a lady to carry your bundles for you, but in America it is supposed to be derogatory and very insulting, like making an indecent noise with your mouth or being asked to debate with a Humanist.)

A constructive critic, on the other hand, seems to be
one who approaches everything he criticizes in a press-
agent mood, armed with good-will and a heart full of
fuzzballs for anything that comes his way. The genial
Prof. Billy Phelps, who enthusiastically compares
"The Mysterious Murder of Mignon Mushhead" and
the New Haven telephone book with the best of Dostoievski and Proust, is accordingly a constructive
critic, while the one who promptly throws "The Mysterious Murder of Mignon" into the cloaca, the mean-
while denouncing Billy for a sweet but effervescent
glow-worm, is a destructive. When it comes to plays,
it is the same. The fact, for example, that I liked "The
Green Pastures" and said as much, giving my reasons
for my taste, made me a constructive critic in my
correspondents' eyes, whereas the fact that I didn't
like such a thing as "Gold Braid" and dismissed it
briefly as garbage made me a destructive. Just where
the sense of either designation lay in these cases, I
cannot see. Everybody liked "The Green Pastures"
and nobody liked "Gold Braid," so where a mere
individual like myself could do anything about constructiveness or destructiveness in either instance is
not too clear. I pointed out why "The Green Pastures"
was a good play, true enough, but where was the constructive criticism in that? I simply pointed out what
everybody else, including the author and producer,
already knew and my remarks, as a consequence, were

gratuitous and superfluous. They amounted to little more than saying that the Chrysler Building had been put up all right. As for "Gold Braid," I said simply that it was rotten and didn't bother to tell why. Say I had said why; what good would it have done? Everybody knew that it was rotten; nobody went to see it; and it closed instanter. Is there anyone so silly as to believe that if I had pointed out its defects with studious critical elaboration, the author would have profited by my constructiveness, gone to the trouble of rewriting his failure and thus added to the season's relatively better dramatic art? More likely, he would simply have put me down for a damned fool. If summarily dismissing such stuff as "Gold Braid" as rubbish constitutes destructive criticism, then announcing in loud, confident tones that a manure bed smells constitutes constructive.

Any critic who goes to the trouble of explaining laboriously why a piece of out-and-out tripe is out-and-out tripe is not a critic so much as he is a pretentious and imbecile space-filler. All the constructive criticism this side of Beverly Hills, Cal., that concerned itself with "The Blue Ghost," "Oh, Professor," "House Afire" and a hundred other such doses of claptrap would not be of half the critical service and merit that the single exclamation "Junk!" is. When a house has smallpox in it, the best and most sufficient thing to do is to tack a card on it reading *Smallpox*.

There is little sense or need to put up a three-sheet explaining in detail what smallpox is, its contagious quality, the desirability of everyone keeping at a safe distance, how the disease can be cured, the diet of the patient, the grief of the latter's parents, the name of the doctor's second cousin, and the number of times a day the nurse (duly stated to be a blonde of petting tendencies or a dark hussy given to gin) has to change the sheets.

What goes by the name of constructive criticism is often something that merely destroys reader interest. It builds up, as the saying goes, but its materials are generally little more than children's blocks, made of cardboard, painted black and labeled *iron*. If drama is improved, it is improved by destructive criticism, or what passes by that name. Constructive criticism gave the American theatre its years of Augustus Thomas, Owen Davis, Charles Klein, David Belasco and George Broadhurst. When destructive criticism invaded the parlor and started in smashing up the cheap gilt thrones and tipping over the playwrights who were sitting grandly in them, it cleared the decks and gave the American theatre the vastly more reputable dramatists that it has today.

§ 21

*Cliché.*— A leading critical cliché has to do with

sudden changes in dramatic character. Such changes, the critics insist, invalidate the outline of the character in point, indicate a defect in the playwright and contrive to make the character dubious and unbelievable. The argument is a familiar one. We have heard it dozens of times. And it persists as one of the most foolish of the many foolish contentions of criticism as that august art is currently practiced. It stems undoubtedly from the ancient dramaturgic text-book rule that a character must remain, throughout the course of a play, more or less a single definite being, keyed to relevantly definite impulses and reactions and recognizable at all times in terms of its psychological and emotional premiss. "Distinct entity" is the phrase, as I recall, that the professors use. Nothing could be richer in bosh. Human nature, unfortunately, is not in the habit of conforming to dramatic text-books. There isn't one of us who doesn't periodically change, if perhaps only for a short time, with the surprising suddenness — to ourselves as well as to others — of a lightning flash. History and one's own house are full of instances. A quirk of mood, an unexpected quirk of mind, a momentary impulse, a jiffyish metamorphosis of self — one of these descends upon the cerebellum or psyche and, *passe-passe*, the trolley-car is off the tracks! Clever playwrights may create characters who remain absolutely and entirely themselves from start to finish, but God is not quite so exact a craftsman.

## § 22

*Demerits.*—One of the chief faults of American dramatic writing lies in the ability of our playmakers to invent excellent minor characters at the expense of leading ones. Plays with minor characters who relegate leading characters to the background and steal the show — to the plays' complete corruption — are common occurrences. The confection of a recognizable minor character is, plainly enough, a relatively easy job compared with the difficult composition of a sustained central and dominating character. The latter task is often beyond the capabilities of our playwrights, whereas the former lies within the narrower confines of those capabilities. A second fault, and a chronic one, is the reliance for comedy not upon the natural turn of dramatic events but upon a number of subsidiary characters more or less arbitrarily introduced into those events, much after the manner in which Mons. Pettipas, the waiter, with his periodic fallings upon his tochus, is introduced into adapted Viennese operetta or the May Vokes kind of servant girl into detective melodrama.

## § 23

*Truth-telling.*—Any vainglorious assumption of immoderate truth-telling is highly offensive to me; I never for a moment desire to posture as a critic who believes that there is any special virtue in unduly forth-right talk, for the man who cherishes that belief is found pretty generally to be a nincompoop who imagines himself a hero on the strength of his bad manners. The truth is a graceful and lovely thing; it may no more be shouted without debauching it than a song by Wolf may be played by a jazz band. The truth should ooze out as softly as Spring from the snow. Yelling it is, in a sense, a form of mendacity.

§ 24

*When Criticism Lapses.*—"After all, what has the grave-diggers' scene to do with the character of Ham-let?" argues George Bernard Shaw in defence of a scene in one of his own plays that has been declared completely irrelevant to the character of his pro-tagonist.

Is it possible that Shaw has lately become as de-ficient a critic as a dramatist? That the grave-diggers' scene has its share in the creation of Hamlet's charac-ter should be plain to anyone. It points Hamlet's under-current of sentimentality and of tender regard for the traditions in his line: "Has this fellow no feeling of his business, that he sings at grave-making?" It points his combined cynicism, fatalism and derisory humor in the speeches over the skulls. It points his gift of sarcasm in the line: "I think it (the grave) be thine, indeed, for thou liest in it." It points his contempt for democracy in his sneering speech, "The age has grown so picked that the toe of the peasant comes so near the heel of the courtier, he galls his kibe." It even establishes his debated age in the observations of the first clown that he became a grave-digger "on the very day that young Hamlet was born" and that "I have been sexton here, man and boy, thirty years." And so on.

The student of criticism is often entertained by similar follies on the part of professional critics, high and low. Much of the disesteem into which criticism has fallen is due to its promulgation, in over-confident and decisive tones, of ideas and doctrines that even the least of laymen readily perceives to be faulty, and not only faulty but often ridiculous. Criticism is used to speaking in a voice of finality, for only by speaking so may it attract the attention that is necessary to its very life. In the business of creating an impression, it frequently sacrifices truth to half-truth. In its effort to make itself heard, it often shouts so loudly that it dizzies itself and staggers grotesquely. Thus, for example, we engage C. E. M. Joad announcing, "The great artist is much too absorbed in what he has to say to care overmuch about how he says it." When a critic of Mr. Joad's otherwise high intelligence says any such thing, mockers of the critical art may be forgiven their smiles. The great artist frequently has nothing to say, or at best very little; it is, he realizes, how he says it that makes him a great artist. Toward the care, eloquence and beauty of its saying he devotes his entire effort. It is the inferior artist who is so absorbed in what he has to say that he does not care overmuch how he says it. The difference is the difference between Shakespeare and Brieux, Joseph Conrad and Upton Sinclair, Franz Schubert and George Antheil.

Misgiving must also set in when Ernest Boyd, generally one of the shrewdest and ablest of critics, writes, "He (Strindberg) was essentially a man without the faintest trace of humor." That Mr. Boyd has here permitted himself to succumb to the Strindberg critical stencil is only too apparent. One may refer him, for instance, to "Happy Peter," a satire on the pompousness of provincial authorities which, resembling in part Ibsen's "An Enemy of the People," has twice the humor of Ibsen. One may also refer him to portions of "The Spook Sonata," to various passages in the short stories and dream plays, to parts of the dialogue (*vide* "Creditors") in the short plays, etc. "As for the German authors of the first rank whose hands are still innocent of American gold," he further writes, "to enumerate them would be to produce a list of names whose English equivalents would be: Arnold Bennett, John Galsworthy, George Gissing, George Moore, D. H. Lawrence, *viz.* Theodor Fontane, Otto Julius Bierbaum, Otto Flake, René Schickele, Alfred

Döblin." The listing of Schickele as the equivalent of
George Moore—to select but one item—surely brings
the critic to the necessity of considerable adroit explanation. When Hilaire Belloc, to continue, says,
"The maintenance of tradition supports the mind in
its extravagance and even its vagaries, and most of
all in its creative impulse. It is the abandonment of
tradition which makes for sterility and death"— when
Mr. Belloc writes thus, one may inquire just how the
abandonment of tradition has made for the sterility
and death — to say nothing of the end of the creative
impulse in modern literature — of Marcel Proust,
James Joyce and Bernard Shaw. It is evident that,
had he been in active critical practice at the time, Mr.
Belloc would have pronounced the immediate doom
of Ibsen. "There is nothing so drearily alike," he
proceeds, "as your modern pornographic novels, principally written by maiden ladies." Where did the nonsensical idea, shared by Mr. Belloc, that our pornographic novels are written principally by old maids
originate? For every dirty novel written by a maiden
lady there are a dozen written by men, married or
divorced women, and flappers. Look over the records
in England and America and observe for yourself.
Mr. Belloc has evidently gained his critical information from the comic papers. "There is much more mul-
tiplicity in one landscape of Poussin, or one lyric of
Keats, or one sonnet of Ronsard than in the whole

mass of the modern revolt put together," he goes on. This is such an obviously silly statement that it calls for no comment.

George Santayana publishes the following: "Few of us can endure the truth. Nietzsche once stated as the great question of the future whether mankind could indeed bear to know the truth and face it. He himself often could not, and most of mankind likewise turns away. Finally, by agreeing to recognize something else as truth, human science is often transformed into a comfortable philosophy. Happily, this is not the case with the recent book by Mr. Walter Lippmann, 'A Preface to Morals.' Mr. Lippmann not only believes that mankind can endure the truth; he has proved it in a measure by the acceptance which his book has had in America." What does Mr. Santayana mean by "acceptance"? And how does that "acceptance" prove even in a measure the contention that mankind, specifically American, can endure the truth? The circumstance that a book has had a wide sale does not necessarily indicate that its readers agree with its doctrines, endorse them, accept them, or are able even to endure them. Sinclair Lewis' "Elmer Gantry" sold very much more widely than Lippmann's book, but very few of its readers accepted its particular truths and were able to stomach them. Lippmann's book was "accepted" by certain professional critics as it was "rejected" by others. Perhaps not one layman out of every hundred who read it could understand it sufficiently either to accept or reject its tenets.

Professor Irving Babbitt, the Humanist Krishnamurti, declares, "If Mr. Theodore Dreiser, author of 'The "Genius",' had set forth his views of originality in Germany about 1775, they would have been wrong, but they would at least have had a semblance of novelty. As it is, it is hard for a person even moderately versed in literary history to read these views without yawning." What, one may ask the Professor, if Goethe, author of "Faust," who flourished in Germany in that century, had set forth his views of originality in Marlowe's England about 1588? "One suspects that Huneker's present admirers would be the first to call him an empty fellow if he had praised Tennyson and Browning instead of Nietzsche and Stendhal." So, Granville Hicks. One suspects that anyone's present admirers would be the first to call him an empty fellow if he had praised Verdi and Gounod instead of Wagner and Beethoven. "The adventures of a soul, even among masterpieces, are worth recording only if the soul itself has some intrinsic worth beyond that lent by enthusiasm and erudition." So, the same critic. From which we may logically deduce that the critical opinions of someone like Mahatma Gandhi are sounder than those of some such defectively souled knave as Samuel Butler or Edgar Allan Poe.

"It takes extreme violence to make us sit up," states Katharine Fullerton Gerould. "No play, no book, no sporting spectacle is going to thrill us unless it can compete with the front page of the newspaper . . . We demand knockouts; we get knockouts; and our emotions are roused by nothing less." Here is journalistic platitude, completely hollow. Among the most popular of recent plays were "Berkeley Square," "The Green Pastures," "Journey's End," "June Moon," "Bird in Hand," "Death Takes a Holiday," "The First Mrs. Fraser," "Uncle Vanya," "Michael and Mary," "Rebound," "Strictly Dishonorable," "Once in a Lifetime," and "That's Gratitude"— not one of which had so much as a trace of extreme violence. Books like "Dodsworth," "The Bridge of San Luis Rey," the Warwick Deeping series of sentimental tales, "The Forsyte Saga," "Death Comes for the Archbishop," "John Brown's Body," "The Story of San Michele" and dozens upon dozens of other relatively placid works have thrilled the country from one end to the other. Madison Square Garden is packed by thousands who apparently enjoy hugely such mild sporting spectacles as six-day bicycle races, hockey games, dancing marathons and the like. And baseball, the national pastime, surely does not make us sit up because of its extreme violence.

The young Mr. Dwight Macdonald crowds the critical rostrum with this ringing address: "Eugene

O'Neill's dodges to escape realism and recapture form in theatrical technique have been varied and ingenious. They include: taking the front wall off a house and revealing its inmates at work and at play ('Desire Under the Elms'), employing dummies to suggest the artificial nature of society ('The Hairy Ape'), putting masks on his characters to indicate their changing states of soul ('The Great God Brown'), and, most famous of all, making his people after every speech tell their real thoughts to the audience ('Strange Interlude'). These are all effective enough theatrically, but there is something childish and in-conclusive about them. It is highly significant that their author has not as yet settled on any one of them to the extent of employing it in even two plays. Ex-periment is good, but not the sort that starts off from the same point in a dozen different directions. To be effective it must be based on the past and continuous with it. O'Neill's experiments in form are unsatisfying and inconclusive because he is trying to create his own forms by himself, something that no dramatist has ever been able to do." Taking the front wall off a house and revealing its inmates at work and at play was no original or ingenious dodge of O'Neill's but was used long before him in "Imprudence," presented more than twenty years ago, in "Johannes Kreisler" and in various other earlier plays, to say nothing of in such antediluvian motion pictures as Tourneur's

"The Hand of Peril." Employing dummies to suggest
the artificial nature of society was a device used
fifteen or more years ago by Eleanor Gates in "The
Poor Little Rich Girl." The use of masks, as in "The
Great God Brown," was anticipated, some centuries
before, by the Japanese, and the articulated thought
device employed in "Strange Interlude," as P. P.
Howe has left-handedly indicated, was used in certain
directions by such playwrights of the nineties as
Pinero. It was also used, much as O'Neill used it, in
a vaudeville sketch called "Overtones," produced a
number of years before "Strange Interlude." Our
critic says that "it is highly significant that their author has not as yet settled on any one of them to the
extent of employing it in even two plays." The first
named device was employed in both "Desire Under
the Elms" and "Dynamo," and the last named in
both "Strange Interlude" and "Dynamo," but that
nevertheless proves nothing. Sophocles employed a
dodge, as our critic would describe it, in the "Philoc-
tetes"— a painted landscape — that he did not repeat in any of his other plays. So, in the "Prometheus,"
did Aeschylus. "Experiment is good," continues the
critic, "but not the sort that starts off from the same
point in a dozen different directions." This may or
may not be true, but what has it to do with O'Neill?
What are the dozen different directions in O'Neill's
case? Our critic makes the mistake of confusing mere

theatrical and stage trickery with dramaturgic form. The device he alludes to in "Desire Under the Elms" is simply a scenic one; it has nothing to do with essential form. The dummies that were used by O'Neill in "The Hairy Ape" were used only in a single brief scene; they did not figure in any sense in any experiment in dramaturgic form. The masks in "The Great God Brown" were incidental to the drama itself; that drama was otherwise largely conventional in form. Only the articulated thought device of "Strange Interlude" was part and parcel of the play's form. "He is trying to create his own forms by himself, something that no dramatist has ever been able to do," concludes our critic, with an air of finality. Has our critic never heard of Ibsen? Or Chekhov? Or Georg Kaiser? Or Ernst Toller?

"Music is the only universal language there is," proclaims Prof. William Lyon Phelps. "If one desires to read Goethe or Tolstoy or Ibsen in the original, one must learn German, Russian or Norwegian. But Beethoven and Tchaikowski and Grieg wrote their masterpieces in the same tongue!" So far as the universal language of music goes, one may suggest to the critic the spectacle of a German audience listening to Chinese music and of a Chinese listening to Richard Strauss. One of the leading critics of the *New Free man* declares, "No critic, historian, biographer has any business fumbling at what goes on in his own time, for in the first place he can make no judgment of it that is worth anything." A suggested reading course for this particular critic might be Shaw, Siegfried, Wassermann, Keynes, Ellis, Ellwood, Russell, Wieth-Knudsen, A. Morgan Young, Walter Burr, A. F. Legendre, *et al.* "If one must seek for flaws in Gamaliel Bradford's method — or, at least, his own handling of the method he has created — it may be that a slight uneasiness, a qualified approach, a playing down, as it were, of the sexual element in the lives of his subjects is to be suspected. But in a civilization where sex is so overplayed, where it is so confidently set forth as the motivating cause of every gesture of bewildered man, perhaps this is not so heinous an offence against complete veracity." Thus, Herbert Gorman, the Humanist bellboy. Despite the lamentable overplaying of sex in our civilization, it is difficult to see how the playing down of sex in the lives of such of Mr. Bradford's sexualists as Ninon de Lenclos, Madame de Maintenon, Madame Guyon, Mademoiselle de Lespinasse, Catherine the Great, George Sand and Sarah Bernhardt can be anything other than a heinous offence against complete veracity. As well — because of the lamentable overplaying of hypocrisy in our civilization — condone an adaptation of "Tartuffe" with the hypocrisy of the character quietly glossed over.

"Jazz," writes Sigmund Spaeth, "will remain a

treatment, rather than an element, even when disguised by the veneer of respectability, and against its on-slaughts the mighty fortresses of Bach, Beethoven and Brahms are fairly sure to stand impregnable." With-out wishing to defend jazz, this is nevertheless like saying that the mighty fortresses of Balzac, Flaubert and Zola are fairly sure to stand impregnable against the onslaughts of James Joyce, Ernest Hemingway and other such modern erratic but none the less consid-erable talents. Of course they are. But is that any kind of sound criticism of Joyce, Hemingway, *et al*? They, too, are treatment rather than element, like jazz. "As a writer of fiction, Hawthorne was plainly not of the first order; his stories do not enact themselves in the open, in the midst of things, in the sunlight," decrees Prof. Newton Arvin. Say what you will against him, the Professor has at least devised a new critical test for worth. If it turns out to be sound, about half the writers that the world regards as great artists will have to be put down finally as literary failures. "Mr. Squire is old-fashioned, so am I," writes H. M. Tom-linson. "Mr. Squire voices what many of us feel about the new style of the latest school of writers. The predilections of these writers, quite properly, give them their style. 'All Quiet' is symptomatic. Its con-tinuous emphasis on matters which once got no more than a passing and discreet reference . . . is only an outstanding example, known to everybody, of a peculiarity that has been noticeable for some years in our new books." Mr. Squire and Mr. Tomlinson are perhaps not so old-fashioned as they imagine. If they were, they would not feel as they do about "the new style of the latest school of writers," nor would they describe its emphasis as being precisely "on matters which once got no more than a passing and discreet reference." Any really old-fashioned person would realize that the emphasis of the latest school of writers is almost effeminately weak when compared with that of Fielding, Smollett, Zola, Gautier and Co.

"Docility and passivity are the outstanding characteristics of American audiences. This is why listening to music, or attending a play, in America is so often a depressing experience. The American idea seems to be that when you set out to look for 'artistic experience,' you pay your money and accept without question what you get for it." Thus, Bruno Kahn, and the old American hoot. Mr. Kahn should travel more. He will find much the same docility and passivity in every country in Europe, Italy alone excepted. As a matter of fact, American audiences are less docile and passive than either English or German, and particularly Austrian. If, in England, Mr. Kahn achieves an intellectual pleasure and finds a lifting of his American depression in the occasional booing of reputable dramatic spectacles by ignorant gallery clerks and shop-girls, that is his business. But if he imagines that

there is a more passive audience in the world than a
German one at a concert, musical festival or play and
if he imagines that a very infrequent hullaballoo at
the Comédie Française over some such war document
as "Le Tombeau Sous l'Arc de Triomphe" or at the
Odéon over some such other as "Alsace" implies a
lack of Gallic docility and passivity on ninety-nine
other evenings out of every hundred, he should book
steamer accommodations immediately and take a look.
One would hardly describe as docile or passive such
American audiences as have performed obscenely at
certain of the concerts given by the so-called revolutionary composers at Carnegie Hall in the last few
years, as have yelled themselves hoarse over a succession of actors from John Barrymore to Siegfried
Rumann and Paul Muni, as have cheered De Pach-
mann and Kreisler and made naughty noises at Benavente's dancing pet, Argentinita, as have remained
standing for twenty minutes at the performances' end
to cheer a succession of plays from "Hamlet" to "The
Green Pastures," as have waxed morally indignant
over "The Captive," "Sex," "Maya" and "Pleasure
Man," and as have on more than one occasion thrown
derisory pennies onto public stages.

"I challenge Count Keyserling to mention one
great man who, if he was an invalid . . . was not
obviously hampered by this invalidism," shouts
Struthers Burt. Acting as the challenged Keyserling's

second, I mention the following more or less great men who were not obviously hampered by their invalidism: Schumann, Rubens, Beethoven, Wagner, Heine, Molière, Strindberg, Ibsen, Swinburne, Rousseau, Chopin, Mozart, Swift, Cervantes, Bach, Weber, Händel, Paganini, Samuel Johnson, Verlaine, Tschaikowski, Joshua Reynolds, Alfred de Musset, Homer, John Milton, De Quincey, William Cowper, Nietzsche, Sardou, Lafcadio Hearn, Mark Twain and Robert Louis Stevenson. " 'La Dame aux Camellias' is mere nonsense if you take it in cold blood. The story is only the mawkish trash about the unsullied hearts of sinful ladies which we nowadays hand over to Hollywood, and which Hollywood reels off incessantly to the world, except, of course, that Hollywood would very soon cure consumption when the time for ending came." So, the ordinarily astute Ivor Brown. Hollywood deserves all that is coming to it, but that does not relieve Mr. Brown of the error of talking nonsense. "La Dame aux Camellias" was produced in Hollywood and the consumption was not only left in it but was liberally embellished with realistic hemorrhages. "La Bohême" was also produced in Hollywood and the consumption death scene photographed with twice the realism it has ever been allowed on the stage. "What used to be called theology is being discussed almost as hotly as Prohibition in the smoke of after-dinner cigars," writes the Abbé Ernest Dimnet.

The reverend Abbe, it is plain, apparently suffers
from most men's delusion that their own particular
trade is paramount in every one's else interest. A
cigar smoker of parts and a proficient diner-out, it
has been my observation that the concern with theology to which the reverend Abbe refers is directly
associated with Prohibition and consists largely in
the use of the Saviour's name as an ejaculation and
in that of the Almighty in conjunction with damns.

A critical Solon of the New York *World* preaches
as follows: "The trouble with American drama, if one
may pick a flaw in so lovely a creation, is that it is not
about anything. Where drama in other countries reflects the current thought in many fields, our drama
reflects no thought whatever; it is celebrated for its
lack of ideas, even boastful of it, and goes its undenia-
bly charming way dedicated to the theory that its main
business is entertainment. And it is quite easy to see
how it got this idea into its head. Here, the dramatic
capital of the country, and the intellectual capital, and
the industrial capital, and the commercial capital,
which is to say New York, are remote from the political capital, which is to say Washington. And it is the
political capital, for some reason, which gives life to
the movements started in the other capitals; which
causes them to seem important, and perhaps ominous,
and hence endows them with some vitality when they
reach the stage." The Pulitzer prize for booby criti-

cism should be awarded, on this count, to the late Mr.
Pulitzer's own paper. Manchester is remote from
London and the Manchester school of drama has reflected the current British thought in many fields.
Munich is remote from Berlin and the drama that has
come out of Munich has done the same in a German
direction. O'Neill, grantedly the only American
dramatist who reflects any thought whatsoever, writes
his plays in Provincetown, Bermuda and France, and
comes to New York about once in every two years and
then for only a few days. Washington, the political
capital, contains many hopeful playwrights, not one
of whom has ever written a play with an idea in it
above the I. Q. of a paperhanger. All those that I
have seen or read have dealt with drawing-room chit-
chat, bootlegger melodrama or boudoir monkeyshines. What is more, the majority of American plays
that have even the faintest trace of ideational content
always fail miserably when they are shown in Washington. What the political capital wants, according
to the statistics, are leg shows. Mrs. Horniman's theatre in Manchester and the many theatres in the German
provincial towns have challenged the London and
Berlin theatres respectively. Most of the important
contributions to modern drama have had no more
relation to the political capital of the nation of their
birth — ideationally, psychically, geographically or
generically — than most of the unimportant ones.

"Because these (social, political, economic and theological) are the very problems which concern Shaw and the fact that Shaw was aware of them when he was a critic of the theatre, they gave body and substance to his reviews." Thus, Gilbert Seldes. What gave Shaw's reviews body and substance was, very simply, his knowledge of theatre and drama. Social, political, economic, and theological problems do concern Shaw, but they concerned him little as a dramatic critic. Mr. Seldes will certainly have to strain his eyes to discover any serious consideration of them in the two volumes of "Dramatic Opinions and Essays."

"The most notable aspect of Nietzsche's writing technically is its lack of structure," oracularizes Mr. C. A. Tacke, when the most notable aspect of Nietzsche's writing technically happens to *be* its structure. The form is perfectly suited to the subject matter. Consider, for example, "Thus Spake Zarathustra." The circumstance that much of Nietzsche's writing is in the form of superficially isolated paragraphs seems to lead the gentleman to imagine that the sum of that writing is not structurally ordered and stylistically compact. "What the average man now wants is the large-scale production and wide diffusion of science, art, music, literature . . . the best to be had; and he is going to get them and to glorify wholeheartedly the heroes of culture who provide them for him," wrote and prophesied Stuart Sherman. What the average man now wants, at the moment of writing, of the best to be had is, according to verified statistics, in science, the radio; in art, lithographs of Greta Garbo; in music, Rudy Vallée's "I'm Just a Vagabond Lover"; and, in literature, Chick Sale's "The Specialist." "No man can know poetry and the truth," believes E. W. Howe. The ancient fallacy. There is as much truth of one sort in Dante, Shakespeare and Walt Whitman, for example, as there is of another in Spinoza, Schopenhauer and a dozen Euckens and Bergsons. In "Science and Marriage" we find Prof. Heinrich Hertwein writing, "I can recommend a marriage between persons belonging to opposing types as being ideal. There will be no quarrels. All will be peace and harmony. The loveliest and brainiest children will issue from such unions. If this is accepted as a rule of guidance, the human race will be the gainer." For instance, George Sand and Dudevant, Shelley and Harriet Westbrook, Sir William Hamilton and Emma Lyon, and Mr. and Mrs. Leonard Kip Rhinelander.

Writing in "The Core of D. H. Lawrence," Mr. Thomas Seltzer, constituting himself a publisher-critic, projects this philosophy: "I know well that an author is his own worst critic." It is perhaps not to be unexpected that a publisher should believe and express such nonsense. There are, of course, some authors, chiefly of the species jitney, who believe that everything they write is very good, but the average reputable author pretty generally has a very fair idea as to the merits or demerits of what he produces. Naturally, he isn't ass enough to tell his publisher that his work isn't up to standard when it isn't, for the simple and obvious reason that he regards his publisher purely as a business man and salesman and doesn't want to discourage him from pushing his book and making it sell. But the author himself, though he keep it a secret, usually knows what is what about his work. Simply because he doesn't take his publisher into his confidence, for the reasons noted, the legend that he is his own worst critic has persisted among publishers. For every worthwhile author who has mistaken the quality of this or that work of his, we have and have had a dozen who have soundly appraised the virtues or lack of virtues of what they have done. That the critics sometimes disagree with them does not necessarily mean that the critics are right. And as for the critical talents of publishers, let us not forget that the best of the latter are firmly convinced that a book that sells must inevitably be better than one by the same author that doesn't. Mr. Louis Bromfield, constituting himself in turn a novelist-scenarist-critic, has this to say: "There is also an inescapable consciousness of legions of morons, cretins and near-illiterates in America, England, Germany, Java, Iceland and Italy who must always be thought of whenever you undertake anything. There are always these in Hollywood peeping over your shoulder, for there is very little evidence of effort to lift up the benighted. It is all the other way about — a leveling-down process, a search for the way to make things easy for the stupidest mind. That is odd, too, in view of the fact that the most successful moving pictures — like 'The Covered Wagon,' 'The Big Parade,' 'Bulldog Drummond,' 'Disraeli,' 'The Street of Chance' and dozens of others have been also the intelligent and somewhat experimental pictures." Just where Mr. Bromfield detects intelligence in the exceptional pictures he names, I should like to have him tell us. "The Covered Wagon," aside from its spectacular views of the wagon trails, was nothing but the yellow-back of the hero and villain making eyes at the same girl. "The Big Parade" had some good low comedy, such as showing a cutie surprising a couple of soldiers in the altogether and various pleasantries in a manure pile, but its intellectuality otherwise was somewhat elusive. "Bulldog Drummond" was a cheap detective story and "The Street of Chance" an idiotic paraphrase of the Rothstein murder case. "Disraeli" was simply the play of the same name more or less literally made into a talkie, with its worst parts added by the movie director.

In the way of amateur criticism, of which the two foregoing pronouncements are typical, we have many entertaining examples. Thus, for instance, Stewart

Beach, editor of the *Theatre Magazine*: "This leads directly to the most pressing problem which the theatre faces today . . . Not only in America but in foreign countries as well there are few dramatic authors to whom we may periodically look for plays which are significant and important contributions to our understanding of the world we live in." What with Hauptmann, Shaw, Galsworthy, Werfel, Schnitzler, Pirandello, O'Neill, O'Casey, Dunsany, Donnay, Rivas, Lenormand, Toller, Lennox Robinson, Chiarelli, Sologoub, Benavente, Bruno Frank, Hasenclever, Kaiser, Yeats, etc., the problem is no more pressing than it has been in many past ages. Thus, in further instance, Robert E. Sherwood: "Mr. Tomlinson is a pipe-smoking author, and therefore apt to be calm, reflective, impersonal and tiresome. The glowing briar seems to create a mood of philosophic abstraction which is not always as gratifying to the reader as it is to the writer. However, when Mr. Tomlinson's pipe goes out, and serves only as something on which to clamp his teeth, his detachment vanishes and the liquid fire of compassionate anger flows through his pen." Mr. Sherwood, it appears, has yielded to an item in the American Credo: that pipe-smoking induces a mood of detached calm and reflection whereas cigar or cigarette-smoking induces one of relative nervousness and impatience. Where and how the legend started is difficult to make out. The

Irish, a race of clay-pipe puffers, are the most bellicose living. The farmer, given to the corn-cob pipe, is the loudest arguer around the stove in the corner grocery store. It is the cigar-smoker who is generally found to be the calm, cool and reflective fellow. Few good poker players smoke pipes. Thus, in still further instance, that indefatigable critical volunteer, Mr. Otto Kahn: "There is only one thing the matter with George Gershwin — he has not learned to cry. I only hope he meets a woman who will turn him down." The profound philosophy of musical composition as expounded by the patron saint of the Metropolitan Opera House!

Editorial criticism in our magazines and newspapers, as already indicated, is often rich in dubiousness. In the *American Mercury*, we strangely encounter this: "They (the state censor boards) allow vulgarity and sickly sentimentalism, but forbid the slightest trace of realism in the few good movies that come their way." They forbid nothing of the kind, painful as it is to have to admit it. From the child-birth episode in "Way Down East" to the Zolaesque realism of "Greed," from the Grand Guignol realism of the decapitation and disemboweled soldier episodes in "Intolerance" and "Hearts of the World" to the realistic amatory and seduction scenes in "The Patriot" and "A Woman of Affairs," from the realistic concupiscence of "The Merry Widow" to the violent realism of "The Sea Beast," "Moby Dick" and "China

Express," the liberality of the abused censors has been disturbingly apparent. In the New York *World*, we encounter such things as this: "One of the nightly radio programs in Porto Rico, as published in *El Regionalista*, one of the journals of the island:

### PRIMERA PARTE

1. *"I Am Living With Memories," vals.*
2. *"Recuerdos y Quimeras" (a petición), danza.*
3. *"That's You, Baby," fox trot.*
4. *"Impere," danzón.*
5. *"One Alone," fox trot.*
6. *"Pombo y Bolado," paso doble.*

### SEGUNDA PARTE

1. *"Marie," vals.*
2. *"Alma Sublime," danza.*
3. *"Júrame," danzón.*
4. *"Siren Dream," fox trot.*
5. *"Gracia y Belleza," paso doble.*
6. *"Walking With Susie," fox trot.*
7. *"Sara," danza.*

"All that we can say about this is that if making Porto Ricans into good Americans has brought them to this, then it is time to haul down the flag!" Brought the Porto Ricans to what? What is so dreadful about the program? It was very plainly designed merely as a dance program. Would the *World* ask Porto Ricans or anyone else to dance to Beethoven, Brahms and Bach? I'll gladly pay the necessary admission fee to watch the *World* critic glide around the floor with his girl to the tune of, say, the Ninth Symphony.

§ 25

*The Foreigner and America.*— The business of publishing books on America by foreigners continues apace, presently running second only to the publishing of that species of novel by Americans which opens: "Mazie wiped the last greasy dish on a dirty towel and began the ritual of washing Joe's socks." During the last few years I have read what seems to be a comprehensive library of these alien impressions of the Republic and its denizens, the confection of Englishmen, Frenchmen, Italians, Swedes, Germans, Spaniards and apparently everyone else in the Eastern hemisphere, save only Central African colored gentlemen. In the lot there have been two and only two books that were even passably interesting — those of Siegfried, the Frenchman, and Spender, the Englishman — and these two were often as obvious as wet water, said very little that everyone had not heard before and were generally inferior to even certain second-

rate books on America and Americans that have been
written by Americans.

The praise that such relatively better-grade treatises
by foreigners invariably gets is critically empty. It is
based not upon their accurate and original research,
impression and deduction, but almost wholly upon
the foreigners' coincidence in and echo of what is
already clearly known here of this country. The circumstance that a foreigner has perceived what every
intelligent American well knows is believed to be the
ground for eulogy of him, and not only for eulogy but
for enthusiastic tribute to his gifts for immensely acute
penetration, clear and original insight and even high
sociological philosophy. Yet all that the moderately
intelligent American discovers in the volumes in point
is a mirror once again held up to books on the same
subject written by Americans, with nothing that is
fresh and new in the way of observation and nothing
that is fresh and new, or even particularly sound, in
the way of deductions from that observation. There
is more truth about America in even such a book as
Charles Merz's "The Great American Band-Wagon"
than in two dozen of the customary books by aliens.
There is a hundred times more vivid and accurate a
picture of Americans in almost any novel by Sinclair
Lewis than you will find in any portentous tome —
with the single obvious exception — written by a foreigner in the last fifty years. And there is a thousand

times more common-sense and information in a book like the Lynds' "Middletown" than you will discover in anything written about America abroad in the last century.

Reducing the bulk of the alien treatises to their simplest terms, one comes upon banality thrice banal: that the American is always in a hurry; that the salient mark of the United States is its exaltation of the business man; that money is the first goal of the American; that the democratic form of government obtaining in America has many flaws; that the American, now that he has come into riches, is learning how to play; that "far too little of the brains and character of the country is going into its public affairs"; that "the majority of Americans seem to be convinced that if only they stick to business everything else will cure itself"; that "the American and Canadian peoples have come now to the era of good feeling, mutual respect and thorough understanding"; that a man living in Chicago does not speak English like a man living in Liverpool; that Billy Sunday and Aimée McPherson are phenomena peculiar to America and could be found nowhere else; that the New York night-court is very interesting and amusing; that Prohibition has not been a success in America and that the well-to-do have all they want to drink — and some very tasty brands, too; that way down deep in America there is an ideal; that there are possible causes for a war between Great

Britain and the United States and that, if it comes, the
Pacific will in all likelihood be the theatre of opera-
tions; that the Germans are none too well informed
about Americans or their culture and read Upton Sinclair and Jack London in preference to Dreiser and
Cabell; that "there is an appalling standardization
and mechanicalization of American life" and that "all
the finer values have been subordinated to mob no-
tions of Success"; that "capitalism rides in the saddle
in the United States"; that "for all the understanding
between nations, the inevitable tangle of economic
forces and psychological motives will bring about
misunderstanding"; that "there is something un-
healthy about American prosperity"; that "instead of
saying that the American worker has a high standard
of living it is nearer the truth to say that he has a high
standard of spending; it is made easy for him to
gratify every passing want; but is it comfort to have a
player-piano and be unable to pay the grocer's bill?";
that "the concentration of power in America rests in
the hands of Wall Street"; that the American girl is
very resourceful and is physically attractive but a
bit hard; that the skyscrapers "are like giants raising
their heads into the skies"; that Federal aid in the
way of subsidies stimulates state interest and state
activity and brings about a certain degree of uniform-
ity without ignoring differences in local needs; that
everybody in America seems to own a radio, a phono-

graph and a Ford; and that the war psychosis still
continues to make genuine understanding between
Europe and America impossible, but that time and
education will help.

When these alien views of the United States are not
absurdly platitudinous, they are often strikingly defective. They are accurate enough when they describe
such things as the Chicago stock-yards, the hospitality
on tap in Richmond, the black-and-tan joints in Harlem and the good-looking shoes and stockings that
even American shop-girls wear, but they are often far
from pointed in their observation of somewhat more
esoteric phenomena. By way of general illustration, I
point to "Through English Eyes," one of the better
of the foreign books and the work of the Spender
already alluded to, J. A., until eight years ago the
able editor of the *Westminster Gazette*. It is Mr.
Spender's observation that since the business man is
unduly exalted in America, even above the statesman,
public affairs in America are left to men of inferior
brains. Aside from the painfully obvious fact that,
since we have no statesmen worthy of exaltation, the
American business man — the Kohinoor of his kind
— inevitably and quite naturally gets the *Kudos* that
the non-existent statesmen might get, we engage the
second fact that the American business man gets his
share of what Mr. Spender calls exaltation not merely
because he is an excellent business man but, more

importantly, because as an excellent business man he figures so largely in America's public affairs. What is thus true of the United States is quite as true, on a somewhat lower scale, of present-day Germany. Some of the best brains of American business are found closely interwoven with public affairs. There is no need to catalogue names; they are immediately recognizable. Politics and government in the United States are today purely a business matter, and correctly so. We are the world's bank. We have infinitely less need of Gladstones and Winston Churchills than of Mellons and, if God had been more just, Raskobs. Maybe the next Mr. Balfour who comes over here on a Mission will not find a hard-boiled business man so easy to fool as a Wilsonian pseudo-statesman.

## § 26

*Concerning Censorship.*— The one big unanswered question concerning censorship as we engage it in this day and hour is this: why is it that that censorship, designed by its own admission to safeguard the young, the susceptible and the ignorant, four times out of five disports itself not in that quarter at all but exercises itself sedulously against institutions and works whose appeal is directly and almost entirely to unsusceptible and intelligent adults? A scrutiny of the subjects of censorship suppression in the United States during the last ten years discloses a preponderance of such subjects that by no stretch of the human imagination may be considered as even remotely to the taste and understanding of the young and ignorant and that, by their very nature, call for an educated, intelligent and sophisticated audience. Irrespective of the artistic value or lack of value of these subjects, it will certainly be granted that such works as James Joyce's "Ulysses," Radclyffe Hall's "The Well of Loneliness," Cabell's "Jurgen," Dreiser's "The 'Genius'," George Moore's "A Story Teller's Holiday" and Sherwood Anderson's "Many Marriages" can have small interest for the unintelligent, whether young or old, and must remain, for all the possible curiosity of the latter, very difficult of reading and assimilation for them, and largely unintelligible. It requires a proficient fancy to imagine a school-girl or a school-boy wading through the literary intricacies of any one of them. Yet it is the untutored, inexperienced and susceptible youngsterhood of the land that invariably in such cases provides censorship with its loudest court-room indignation and argument.

No man, not a lout, contends that the selling of dirty postcards and cheap pornography to the impressionable young should not be frowned upon and put an end to by the police, if they can find enough time for the job from their chief business of selling tickets to police charity balls and the like, or by the censors if the police are too busy in that direction. Nor can any rational person greatly work himself up over the suppression of photographs of naked burlesque show queens palmed off as art studies, or over the censorship of such pornographic trash as "Fleurette's Adventures in the Harem" and "Green Girls in Paris." No doubt the ignorant and the young do get ideas looking at such photographs and reading such stuff, since neither the looking nor the reading imposes any strain upon their undeveloped faculties. But just how a young idiot, or an adult one, for that matter, is supposed to be morally damaged by such higher literature as I have named, which demands a considerable measure of sophisticated intelligence and patience for its mere perusal, is hard to figure out.

A possible reason for the professional moralists' crusade against works of the kind presents itself. The suppression of French postcards, "Only a Boy," "art" magazines and other such out-and-out rubbish, being reasonable, naturally attracts neither opposition nor notice further than a half-stick buried in the newspapers to the effect that agents of this or that anti-vice organization descended upon Moe Schafskopf's little cigar store near Public School No. 18 and arrested Moe for selling a picture of Gaby Plaisir, of the Moulin Rouge, in one of her more emotional moments. But the attempted or negotiated suppression of a work meant for the adult understanding, whether it be critically praiseworthy or not, equally naturally arouses the notice and opposition of adult and understanding men and women, many of them conspicuous in the arts and in national life, and the newspapers as a consequence may be expected to spread themselves in the situation. This newspaper publicity attracts to the moralists' organizations the notice necessary to their very life and maintenance, for sustaining funds are not born out of the dark but out of the limelight. And it is this publicity that they must get by hook or crook, or perish. No moralist organization can work *in camera* for long and survive. The New York Anti-Vice Society has already found that out. For a short time, due to an agreement with the District Attorney's office, it was brought to conduct its work under cover, only to learn that its exchequer was rapidly and sadly going to pot. But, though the agreement with the District Attorney's office may still be in effect, it has lately again removed the diaper from its face, come out into the open and, by way of attracting the all-important money, made the necessary public noises with the resulting valuable journalistic publicity.

It is not a matter of safeguarding morals so much as it is a simple and comprehensible matter of business. Had God had a distaste for me and inculcated me at birth with a nosey moralistic nature, I should undoubtedly have supported myself in the world by the same technique that these less fortunate fellows

are currently driven to. I would not be wasting my
time and starving to death hunting around for copies
of "One Voluptuous Night" and "A Débutante's Adventures with the White Slavers," but I'd get on my
toes, prepare to jump upon the Dreisers, Cabells,
Joyces, Schnitzlers and Moores, arouse the indignation of reputable publishers, writers, editors and lawyers, get a lot of excellent publicity and so make
myself heard of and draw in the easy money. The
moralists are not fools; they know which side of the
bread has the butter on it; and so they shrewdly do
that very thing.

§ 27

*Men Without a Country.*— More and more it becomes plain that in the United States there is coming
into being a steadily augmented body of Americans
who have been deprived of the America that they were
born into and that once they came to know and love
and who, bewildered and lost in a new, strange nation, find themselves in the position of expatriates in
their own country. That country, long their happy
home, has in later years taken on the aspect of an
alien land and in it they find themselves dislocated,
suspect, at sea and uncomfortable. Its people and their
ways are not those they used to know; its conduct is
a conduct that they cannot understand; its laws and

the administration of those laws are offensive to them; and their United States, the United States of Washington and Jefferson, of Lincoln and Grover Cleveland and even of Roosevelt, is a United States now only by pseudonym.

These expatriates in their own country are neither professional radicals nor soap-box indignantos, neither alarmists nor adult college-boy dissenters, neither superficial dilettantes nor philosophical reds. They are, by the old American standards, the better and more intelligent and more dignified class of Americans, Americans of standing in the professions, the arts, the sciences, finance and society. They are Americans of understanding and poise, with a sound and sober sense of fairness and justice, and of decency and honor. Against this new, strange nation that they have suddenly discovered themselves in, against its new mob and its mob's new chieftains, against its tide of commonness, cheapness, vicious dishonesty and un-Americanism, they stand aghast, helpless as men without passports and barred by their very Americanism — the Americanism of their youth — from sympathy and assimilation, and from life, liberty and the pursuit of happiness. The America of today is a gigantic Left Bank whereon, far from their old home and homesick, they are driven to cower before the persistent and galling forces of spiritual extradition.

It isn't that these expatriates wish to be expatriates;

they simply can't help being what they are. To be
other than they are would be to confess themselves
un-American by the precepts of Americanism that they
were brought up according to and in which they were
educated and trained. They still believe in the old
Constitution of the United States, now debilitated and
emaciated by political disease. They still believe in
the old American Bill of Rights, now indistinguishable
from a Chinese laundry bill. They still believe in
American justice, not in the Sacco-Vanzetti brand;
and they still believe in American fair play, not in
the Mooney kind of play. They still believe in free
speech for Americans and not in the Wilsonian doctrines that have survived their sponsor. They still
believe in the decency of American women and not
in the prosecution and conviction of an honorable
and intelligent mother who tells her children how to
order their lives, whether sexually or otherwise. They
still believe that the relations of a doctor and his
patients are confidential and not open to any raiding
policeman with an excessive itch for promotion. They
still believe that censorship motivated by corruption,
political or individual, is not to be tolerated, and they
still believe that a man's house is his castle — as his
boyhood house was — and not liable to invasion by
any blackguard in a blue suit. They still believe that
an American House of Representatives that loudly
applauds the murder of a boy as justified by the cir-

cumstance that the boy was driving a Ford alleged to contain a couple of cases of beer is not a House of Representatives that represents them. They still believe in gentlemanliness and in chivalry and not in shunting off to Ellis Island any Englishwoman, with or without a title, who once has sinned against convention.

They believe, these expatriates, that the great-grandson of Gouverneur Morris speaks for them when he says that this is no longer the America of his great-grandfather and that, more, it is no longer his as he was taught to know it: that he finds himself a strange and lonely man in a strange and lonely land. They oppose, after Article VIII of the old Constitution, the imposition of excessive fines and the infliction of cruel and unusual punishments; they cannot persuade themselves to regard as just a ten thousand dollar fine and five years in jail for selling a glass of sherry; and they still believe that, by Article IV, no one has a right to paddle their persons after they have said goodbye to friends sailing for Europe. They still believe, with the fathers of their erstwhile country, that their nation should avoid entangling alliances with foreign nations, and that the Monroe Doctrine is a policy of self-defence rather than one of aggression and that it should not infringe upon the independence and sovereignty of other American states. They still believe that the ambassadorial domains of ministers from friendly powers should be inviolate, that the private morals of visitors from foreign lands should be their own affair, and that true idealism and the demand for promissory notes for services rendered in the cause of idealism are hardly compatible.

They believe, too, these isolated American expatriates, that the Daughters of the American Revolution should hardly constitute themselves a censorship body and that the American Legion should hardly constitute itself in turn an adjunct to the Ku Klux Klan. They prefer the old principles of the Grand Army of the Republic, soldiers first and last. They still believe in the preservation of the integrity of the courts and of their officers, and in the simplicity and lack of snobbery of a nation whose secession from monarchy was urged and whose independence was authenticated by farmers, merchants, shoe-makers, printers, planters, sailors and soldiers. They still believe in the democracy of Jefferson and in the humanity of Lincoln and in the brave forthrightness of Cleveland, now no longer existent. They still are opposed to secret treaties, and they still believe that in time of war the interned enemy should be treated after the established principles of war, not like wolves and hyenas. They still believe that the American people, under their Constitution, shall be secure in their papers and effects against unreasonable searches and seizures, that no state shall make or enforce any law which abridges the privileges or immunities of citizens of the United States, and that the rights of the citizens of the United States shall not be denied or abridged on account of race or color.

These men in a country and yet without one no longer have even their flag. Its once proud stars are now so many policemen's shields, and its once proud stripes the insignia of convicts.

§ 28

*Meditation.*— Having looked upon most parts of the world in the forty-odd years that the Lord Almighty has rejoiced the earth with my presence, I come to the conclusion that of all the lands I should like to spend my declining days in, England is the fairest. Though hardly an Anglophile, either by tradition of birth or training, and though doubtless, out of long association, as ineradicably American as any citizen of partly alien blood can be, there is something about England that deeply appeals to me and makes me believe that, for a considerable part of my later years at least, I could be very happy there.

Many men like me, I know, have felt and feel the same way about it, and the reason seems to be simple. The bosh about the pull of the motherland doesn't interest me; if there were any such pull in my case, it would, because of genealogical and cultural influ-

ences, be toward France or Germany. The bosh about
the peace and quiet of English country life with its
inducements in the way of tranquil speculation and
literary enterprise interests me even less. Bernards-
ville, New Jersey, to name a single American locality,
has much the same advantages. The theory that in
England one meets with men and women less given
to hustle and money and more to the finer impulses of
life also fails greatly to impress me; I know a sufficient number of such men and women right here at
home. The fact that one can live more cheaply in England than in America and get twice as much comfort
for the same expenditure is, true enough, attractive
but, in the point I have specifically in mind, relatively
negligible.

That point is this: England is the ideal country in
which to grow engagingly and satisfiedly old. In
America, age is a burden. In Italy, it is a bitter and
regretful challenge. In Germany, it has about it a
trace of assertive resignation. In France, it is a joke.
But in England it is almost a pleasure. No men grow
old so gracefully and so wisely as Englishmen and
it is their country rather than they themselves that
seems to be responsible for the phenomenon. Unlike
the men of other nations, the Englishman doesn't fight
age; he not only accepts it but has the air of welcom-
ing it. In it he sees a fine contentment, a humorous

wisdom and a certain vicarious delight. And his attitude is reflected in his look and the look of the men about him. It would be agreeable to live out one's life in the midst of such men.

# BOOK III: CHRONICLES

## § 1

*The American Dramatist.*— Let us devote ourselves
to a consideration of living American dramatists and
to an effort to ascertain what place, if any, they presently occupy in the theatrical sun.

That O'Neill is the outstanding figure in the catalogue under discussion is now denied only by such
critics as employ the denial, against their honest and
better judgment, to lend to their writings that share of
fillip which always attaches to a marching out of
step. Their insincerity is easily penetrable, for while
they eloquently argue that O'Neill is not the outstanding force, they do not tell us who is. With the production of "Dynamo," a very poor piece of work, the
hostility toward its author and the skepticism over
his hitherto loudly proclaimed talents took on full sail,
and we were entertained by an over-night shifting of
the critical course. Because he had written a bad play,
O'Neill, his antecedent work forgotten, was denounced
as an overestimated and even ridiculous dramatist,
and it was argued that, since this one play was so bad,

doubtless his previous good plays were not really so good as they had previously been thought to be. In this we engaged no novelty, for the tactic is a commonplace one in American criticism, whether literary or dramatic, and familiar to everyone who follows the critical art as it is manoeuvred in God's country.

If O'Neill is not the leader among American playwrights, "Dynamo" or no "Dynamo," it is pretty difficult to make out who the leader is. While it is perfectly true that in one or two of his other plays, as well as in "Dynamo," he has exposed at times a juvenile indignation, a specious profundity and a method of exaggeration that has verged perilously on travesty, he has nevertheless written a number of plays of a very definite quality, a number of plays that outdistance any others thus far written by Americans and, whether in his better work or poorer, shown an attitude and an integrity — to say nothing of a body of technical resource — far beyond those of any of his American rivals. The truth about O'Neill is that he is the only American playwright who has what may be called size. There is something relatively distinguished about even his failures; they sink not trivially but with a certain air of majesty, like a great ship, its flags flying, full of holes. He has no cheapness, even in his worst plays. "The First Man," "Welded" and "Dynamo," for example, are mediocre affairs as drama goes, but in them just the same there

is that peculiar thing that marks off even the dismal
efforts of a first-rate man from those of a second-rate.

To argue that O'Neill, while an American, does
not write strictly American drama, that is, drama that
issues part and parcel out of American life but rather
drama of more or less universal cast, is to beg the
question. Hauptmann, Porto-Riche, Galsworthy, Pirandello, Rostand, Echegaray — for that matter, every
significant dramatist from the Greeks through to
Shakespeare, Molière and Ibsen — has written drama
of similar cast, for all its identification with immediate time and place. So much is the worst kind of
platitude. It is also the most superficial kind of criticism and in O'Neill's case often silly. For certain of
his plays smell of America as pungently as rotten
diplomacy. But, the one way or the other, what
O'Neill has brought to the American drama, aside
from his own contributions to it, is almost more than
anything else precisely what Shaw brought to criticism of the drama: a gift of independence and courage to others. He has shown the aspiring American
playwright that there is a place here for a whole-
hearted integrity in dramatic writing, and that there
is a public here that is generous in its response to it.
He has shown this by patient and often despairing
labor, and by his uncommon personal intrepidity, and
by his forthright denial of the theatre as he found it,
and — with convincing concreteness — by the prac-

ticability of what he dreamed and set out to accomplish and has accomplished. He has, in a word, proved to the American playwright with potential stuff in him that he need not be fearful, as long he had been, of what is foolishly called the literary drama and of what is looked at askance as the drama of limited appeal — and that there is often a much more substantial reward, in terms of the First National Bank, in fine and honest effort than in half-hearted or intrinsically shoddy.

The effect is already observable, not in actual achievement, perhaps, but in the direction that the native drama is going. Playwrights, having gained confidence from O'Neill's success, are beginning to apply themselves to the drama seriously. To anyone whose professional duties bring him into touch with dramatic manuscripts from the four corners of the Great Democracy, the omen is plain. Most of these manuscripts are still pretty bad, but there is an intention in them that was not there before. They are striving for something. They are trying to dig deep, not into the souls of actors dressed as Governors of New York, Pinero actresses dressed as Salvation Army Nells and Supreme Court justices who believe in thought-transference, but into those of men and women out of the soil and the life that they know. They are interested not in the Solon Shingles, Mulberry Sellers and Bardwell Slotes of vaudeville America

or in the Davy Crocketts of ten-twenty-thirty melodrama America but in human beings far removed
from grease-paint and close to the quivering pulse of
that America unillumined by artificial light and un-
adorned with tinsel and false whiskers. Nor has
O'Neill's influence spread merely to these rookies and
the potential figures of our drama of tomorrow. The
spur that he has given to playwrights already in
practice, some of them long before him, is obvious
to anyone who keeps an eye on the theatre. Any number of new men are plainly rowing in his wash, as yet
without much strength but surely in a direction indicated by his compass. And even such playwrights of
an earlier generation as Owen Davis, author of
"Chinatown Charlie" and "Bertha, the Sewing Machine Girl," may be observed pathetically trying to
get in the swim with their "Detours" and "Icebounds."
O'Neill has sounded the new note and if there are
still no dramatic musicians proficient in striking it,
the desire to strike it is evident. That is something.

On a plane different from O'Neill's we find independence and courage pitching themselves no less
into drama and getting rid at one swoop of all the
inhibitions, chiefly of a moral nature, that American
drama since its birth had been heir to. The timidity
that had previously made the native drama fit fare
only for Edwardian wives, sisters and sweethearts has
disappeared, and writers have ceased to be ashamed

of being adults. The day when comedies like Clyde
Fitch's were accepted as clinical studies of the female
of the species on the ground that Fitch knew what
kinds of hats women admired and the French names
for their underwear has been snickered into limbo, as
has the more recent day when Sheldon's plays were
accepted as surgical portraits of the male on the
ground that he didn't make a tough mug speak like a
Harvard graduate and occasionally allowed him a
measure of carbonated biology in the presence of an
inviting female. Our playwrights, even certain of those
of unfortunately minor talent, are more and more,
in the great Dr. Brisbane's phrase, looking nature and
fact straight in the eye. The whilom sentimentality
and equivoque are disappearing, and truth is gradually finding itself in stage surroundings hitherto
strange to it.

That the American drama has thus made big strides
in the last ten or fifteen years surely no one will deny.
That, however, is not the immediate point. The point
is that many of our commentators have become so
excited over the strides that they have lost all sense
of judgment and values and, like youngsters at a
circus parade, so deliriously throw their hats into the
air during the passing of the bespangled goats and
asses that they have no strength left when the elephants
go by. Among the playwrights who are presently
being anointed as men of rare talent we find any num-

ber who are little more than Kleins and Thomases in 1931 clothes. Of genuine profundity and skill they have no more than, and sometimes not even so much as, the third-rate Americans who preceded them; it is simply their trick of rewriting the old plays through the eyes of the modern gin philosophy that deceives their admirers and causes the latter to estimate them in terms of the calendar rather than as dramatic artists. Your average present-day so-called sophisticated critic is beguiled by a play in the degree that its theme pleases him; to its quality as sound dramatic writing he is more or less blindly indifferent. And it is thus that a second-rate play which assures him that adultery, say, is to be taken no more seriously than bean-bag will always get a more laudatory notice from him than a first-rate play which happens to take an opposite point of view.

As examples of playwrights who are currently being eulogized out of all proportion to their actual worth we have such as the Messrs. George Kelly, Philip Barry, Paul Green and Sidney Howard. While freely admitting that one or two of these men now and then show faint signs of merit, any critic with an ounce of discrimination must experience considerable difficulty detecting in any of their plays that which would entitle them to the position which is carelessly being accorded them. Kelly has written just one fairly good play, "Craig's Wife," and even this one fairly good play showed immaturities, among them a tendency toward generalizations from the specific and particularized, that clearly betrayed the amateur. In "The Show-Off" he achieved one amusing character and then took much of the edge off it by inserting it into a banal Winchell Smith script; in "The Torch-Bearers" he simply expanded an entertaining vaudeville sketch of his into a steadily less and less entertaining three-act play; and in both "Behold, the Bridegroom" and "Maggie, the Magnificent" he plainly — even disastrously — proved that true profundity of character is still far beyond his reach. Like the clown who would play Hamlet, Kelly aspires to write Ibsen. Possessing a gift for low humor that should be sufficient unto his pride, he somewhat ashamedly puts it behind him, wipes the flour from his face, takes off his cardboard red nose and his pantaloon costume and, making himself up in Norwegian whiskers, hopes to trick his audiences into the impression that he is a very profound, serious and even mordacious fellow. Attempting vaingloriously to push into the higher circles of drama, he has deserted the lowly but eminently estimable humors that stood him in good stead and has sought to mingle familiarly with themes and ideas far above his station. And, in the attempt, his feet — accustomed to the rougher boards of the vaudeville stage — have slipped on the highly polished floor and landed him humiliatingly upon his ear.

Green, thus far and for all his obvious sincerity, has indicated himself to be merely a weak little trailer after O'Neill. His work exhibits periodic virtues in detail, but not a single play that he has manufactured has got anywhere near its original plan. The ambition is there, but the skill to realize it is still in abeyance. Howard relies for effect upon the cut-and-dried device of taking a familiar theatrical theme and arbitrarily standing it on its head. His plays are at bottom the plays of twenty-five years ago with their coats turned inside out. As for Barry, I can find even less in his work to warrant the prevailing estimate of him than I can find in the case of any of the others named. "You and I," "In A Garden," "The Youngest," "White Wings," "John" and "Hotel Universe" are all completely negligible efforts, and his "Paris Bound" and "Holiday," while pleasant little comedies, are still several notches not only below earlier American comedy writing but even more below certain other American comedy writing being done in his time. But once the reviewers have fastened upon their idols they stick to them like leeches; once they have made up their minds that this or that playwright is a big boy they stick to their decision until hell freezes; and so the trumpets go on blowing after everyone else has rolled over and snored himself to sleep.

While I trust it need not be pointed out that none of these Beckmessers, even, I daresay, in their admirers' estimation, has ever done anything to allow him elbow-room in the same atelier with O'Neill, it may be pointed out, if only by way of showing up the fatuity of their encomiasts, that the best of the efforts of any one of them is distinctly inferior to what has been negotiated by presumably lesser American contemporaries. Kelly has never written a play one-half so sound as Anderson's and Stallings' "What Price Glory?" Barry has not written anything so good as Gribble's "March Hares," or Zoë Akins' "Papa," or Anderson's "Saturday's Children." Howard hasn't come anywhere near a play of the quality of Patrick Kearney's "A Man's Man" or Rita Wellman's "The Gentile Wife." And Green has never got Negroes onto paper so shrewdly as Ernest Howard Culbertson did in "Goat Alley," or as Rapp and Thurman did in "Harlem." What is more, neither Kelly nor Howard, Green nor Barry has so far done a single thing to compare in the way of honest quality with Zoë Akins' "A Texas Nightingale," or George Kaufman's and Edna Ferber's "The Royal Family," or Booth Tarkington's "Clarence," or Vincent Lawrence's "Two Married Men," or Frank Craven's "The First Year," or S. N. Behrman's "The Second Man," or Arthur Richman's "Ambush," or Maurine Watkins' "Chicago." But the new nonsense is in the air; certain playwrights must be singled out regardless to go into the Hall of Fame; give us geniuses or give us death! The Bronson Howards and Hernes and Augustus Thomases and Belascos are no more; new prodigies must be found to take their places and keep the flag flying. Enter, accordingly, the designated dramatic barbershop quartette.

Thus, with O'Neill in a category apart, we come to a study of the American playwright by and large. Here we find actual achievement much less frequently than mere promise. Some of the writers have shown brilliant streaks and have even produced a single play here and there of authentic quality, but they are found to be flash dramatists rather than sustained and have further demonstrated so uneven a purpose that it is hard to deduce their basic dramatic motives. Maxwell Anderson and Laurence Stallings started out, in "What Price Glory?," in fine color but their subsequent collaborations, while not without traces of merit, have come nowhere near their first work. Stallings has apparently given up original dramatic composition and devotes himself periodically to dramatizations of novels, and Anderson, going it on his own, has since the dissolution of the partnership written only one play, "Saturday's Children," that calls for even passing comment. Both these men, singly and in collaborative endeavor, have ability, but neither has held the position hinted at in their first joint effort. Sidney Howard, as I have written, I am able to discern little in. He impresses me as a box-office playwright and little else; a less operatic Edward Sheldon who looks at life with a campus brand of realism and whose work suggests a footman's paraphrase of available O'Neill themes. Howard can write smoothly and he is by no means a cheap-jack, but there is about him the air of a dilettante trying to mingle familiarly with roughneck ideas. He has written some good single scenes, but his plays in their entirety have an amateurish mental ring and an aspect of strained youthful bravado, like little boys trying manfully to smoke their fathers' cigars.

Paul Green, already referred to, has an unmistakable ambition to write reputable drama but, though he works in materials with which he is undoubtedly familiar, he constitutionally looks at them more as a literary man than as a dramatist. He feels his materials, but his materials do not feel him. And since the materials he deals with are purely emotional the plays he writes are chilly with moods beheld but not echoed. Vincent Lawrence, the most gifted of our comedy writers, now and then contrives to go two-thirds of the regulation play distance, but thus far has not succeeded in writing a full-length play that hasn't expired with its second curtain. For two acts he has at times indicated a talent for comedy of very high flavor, but with the dawn of the third acts his wind has given out and his plays have collapsed, like brave kites with insufficient tails. Yet he has a point of view and a writing skill that one day may bring something fully meritorious from him. That he writes truer and more biting dialogue than any other playwright in our theatre is already pretty widely granted. But that he also has the most understanding and unsparing conception of the single subject that interests him — the ramifications of the amorous passion — still remains to be impressed upon those who believe that that analytical art must inevitably speak with a French accent.

My respect for Lawrence is based not only upon his talent for perception, his acute comprehension and his dialogic skill, but — even more — upon his absolute and forthright independence in declining to dramatize his findings in sympathy with the box-office. It would at times be very easy for him to compromise with popular taste in such a way that even his critics would be deceived, as many a finer dramatist has done, but he doesn't seem to be able to discover it in him to do so. With O'Neill, he is the only completely honest playwright that we have. His failure, commercially speaking, is the price of his honesty, for it so happens that the themes he selects, unlike certain of those of O'Neill's, are essentially distasteful to that large majority of the public that, while it may believe in truth, yet prefers to worship it, like God, at a considerable distance.

What keeps Lawrence from being a comic dramatist of real stature is, first, his apparent inability to make his characters refrain from turning actors in the last moments of his plays and, secondly, his occasional in-

validation of his otherwise excellent theses with momentary lapses into dubious philosophies. In the
former regard, his characters now and then suggest
first-rate photographs marred by the circumstance that,
just before the camera exposure has been snapped
shut, a flea has crossed the lens. In the latter, we find
an illuminating example in "Among the Married."
Lawrence, following the impulse of many of our writers of polite comedy, cannot resist the injection into
his work of a dash of generalized immoralizing or of
what may be called amorous etiology. Just as one is
becoming completely persuaded by the successive
after-images of his characters' speech and acts, he per-
emptorily causes one of those characters to stand apart,
metamorphose himself Fregoli-like into Vincent Lawrence, and denaturalize the convincing impression of
the whole by gravely reciting some titbit that Lawrence
has ingested from some sex pundit or other. The titbit
in point not only does not fit itself to Lawrence's theme
but, even if it did, would debilitate it quite as much as
the sudden injection of a "Now, listen!" would weaken
the effect of, say, the Gettysburg Address.

"Among the Married" treats, with generally rare
observation and a faithful ear, of the emotional and
physical relations of the more leisurely yoked. With
a beautiful craft that mimics naturalness so closely that
the dividing line is almost imperceptible, the author
penetrates the exteriors of his characters and from

under their layers of silk and broadcloth slowly fetches
forth the contented unhappiness, the challengeful
peace, the deceitful honesty and all the other paradoxical qualities that squirm with a stinging recognizability
in their typical innards. The dialogue with which he
negotiates this digging for mica is as easy and natural
as if it had been caught by a discriminating and humorous dictaphone; only once during the course of the
play, when he confounds mere speed with nervous impatience, does the talk become theatrical. As for his
characters, they are for the major portion of the evening constantly themselves; their every detail of comportment is that naturally expected of them; they are
not, as is so often the case, characters whose actions,
whatever their thought and speech, suggest that they
are blood relations of some stage director. Only in
their last moments, as remarked, do they slide slightly
from complete recognition.

So much for virtues.

The comedy tells a tale fundamentally familiar to
the theatre since the day of "Divorçons." Hundreds of
distillations have anticked behind the footlights in this
or that guise and here is simply still another edition of
the sauce-for-the-goose-sauce-for-the-gander theme.
Lawrence has removed most of the grease-paint from
the theme as it is habitually treated and gives it the
feel and quiver of life. It is when he insinuates himself
into the play and gives his little lecture that he grieves

the judicious. It is not enough for him to let his characters act naturally; he must explain the causes of their natural actions and in the explaining turn a good playwright into a bad theorist. The leaf that Lawrence has on this occasion taken from some one's else treatise on anatomical arson has to do with man's biological necessity for several women as opposed to woman's need for only one man. Failing to ponder the borrowed doctrine as closely as he scrutinizes the psychical idiosyncrasies of his own characters, he rashly visits it upon those characters, to the ruin of the dramatic integrity of at least one of them, his central woman figure. Nor, which is worse, does he filter the theory through his own clear head and detect it to be the buncombe it is.

The day that a woman as scientifically gifted as Havelock Ellis, say, records her conviction that, while man needs a harem, woman is content with a solitary Sultan, on that day will I put some faith in the dogma hitherto advanced by males alone. In the doctrine as currently promulgated we have man's most sentimental contribution to amorous philosophy: "Ave Maria" in terms of "Don Giovanni." But this is somewhat beside the point. The point is that, buncombe or not buncombe, the tenet is inapplicable, as already noted, to the actions of Lawrence's chief characters. These, the husband and the wife, do not seek physical satisfaction elsewhere, for all their overly assertive say-so, so much as they seek what all such seekers seek, to wit, a kind of sexual Stokowski-ism, or, to put it into simpler terms, that gratification which is nine-tenths romantic and one-tenth physical. It is the adultery that men commit with their ears when they hear a Strauss waltz and that women commit with their eyes when they look at the director of the orchestra. It is this adultery resolved into actuality, often with physical indifference, that is responsible for the collapse of many such marriages as Lawrence pictures. Man, being more romantically and sentimentally minded than woman, is generally the first offender, however much it pains him. It isn't that he is vain and wishes to be a dog with the ladies, as is generally maintained; it is simply that he sees in women the mirage of beauty that women, very much more sagacious, seldom permit themselves to see in men. Women's realistic conception of men is responsible for their relatively greater continence. They generally take out their satisfaction in holding to the illusion of an unattainable male or, if occasionally they take it otherwise, simply for the purpose of forgetting that gnawing illusion for a brief space of time. Men more often, against the pull of their physical impulses, promiscuously commit *crim. con.* with hypothetical female rainbows and then foolishly leave their umbrellas behind them.

That, anyway — if Lawrence will condone my presumption — was his play, even if he did not appreciate the fact and write it into it. The borrowed bogus philosophy that he has pitched into the play that he has actually written has no place in it; his own central woman character plainly does not believe in it for a moment. Everything she does and the way she does it belie Lawrence's visitation of the filched credo upon her. Revenge against her philandering husband is at the bottom of her sexual digression, but not any article in what is called the new morality — most certainly not the article of sexual equality. It is thus that Lawrence's characters of wife and husband suddenly cease being characters and turn play-actors at the very moment of their potentially highest conviction. Both were looking simply for a new thrill, and sex was the smallest part of that thrill. Lawrence himself inadvertently shows this clearly in the reluctance of the husband — after his to him glamorous adventure with the Spanish dancer — to enter into physical relationship with the attractive wife of his neighbor. The fellow is looking not for sexual gratification but for yellow silk, illusion and charm. He is forced into the sex business itself unwillingly.

Lawrence seldom commits such an unhappy psychological error as he has committed in this most recent piece of his. The body of his work is more often original and, in its originality, sound. But, whatever his slips and whatever the possible dubiety of certain of his appropriations from amatory lore, he remains the most observant writer of high comedy that we have on this side of the Atlantic. The great majority of the pursuers of the comic muse other than Lawrence are hashy fellows, either out-and-out box-office solicitors or men with resolve but without the viewpoint, poise and writing skill to execute it.

There was a day when a local critical erythrodermia was induced by the circumstance that the American playwright was too light-hearted a person, one who persisted in avoiding serious themes and in regarding only the trivial and frothy aspects of life. The lament may surely no longer be indulged in. The hundreds of young men and young women whose manuscripts today crowd the producers' and play brokers' mails are apparently intent upon looking on the world as one long succession of funerals, interrupted now and then by the collisions of hearses and the dumping of corpses into public places. For this melancholy business not only the more foolish critics but the numerous little theatres, art theatres, community theatres and theoretically advanced drama guilds are to blame. It is always a conviction of the amateur mind that a bad play that views life soberly is somehow better than an equally bad one that views it lightly. There is something about most humor that seems *infra dignitatem* and just a little cheap to the arty minded and the latter, through their theatrical organizations and by their propaganda, have donkeyishly dissuaded the playwrights of the country from it. The result has been a vain striving on the part of hopeful playmakers toward dramatic profundity, as futile and as empty of fruitfulness as a Dada novel or a prayer to God.

The success of O'Neill has of course been another factor in the encouragement of the young playwright to spill the works and tell all. Countless juvenile as well as adult snatchers at some of O'Neill's glory and royalties have spread themselves over the coastland, determined to plumb the depths but unhappily unequipped with diving suits. To these, some of whom — had it not been for O'Neill — might conceivably in time have developed their lighter competences, comedy is anathema and only a contemplation of the sores and ulcers of life a worthy profession. In their tadpole sobriety, they scribble off a library of balderdash which leans so far backward from humor that it bends in upon itself like a pretzel, and from them, with the help and assistance of the art theatre groups and misguided producing adolescents, we get the current liberal smear of pseudo-profound poppycock dealing with burnt-cork Spinozas, flapper Margaret Sangers, Strindbergian street-walkers and doughboy Bismarcks. The writing of comedy — that is, comedy in the better sense — has been discouraged, strangely enough even in quarters that might properly impress one as being unsusceptible to influence, and from such quarters what comedy we accordingly receive discloses corrupt-

ing traces of the pervading itch for philosophical
speculation. It is difficult to think of more than one or
two comedies written hereabouts recently that have
not at one or another point in their action becheesed
themselves with small second-hand doses of Schopenhauer, Nietzsche, Ellen Key, Havelock Ellis or Oswald
Villard. Comedy for comedy's sake is forgotten in the
imbecile impulse to make it something more than
comedy and in the author's eagerness to establish himself as something of a great thinker to boot. There
must be a metaphysical theme song, a shadow of what
is called purpose, a measure of what is called weight.
Laughter that springs from a sound comic viewpoint
filtered through engaging literary and dramatic skill
is not enough; there must also be A Note.

Philip Barry, alluded to before, displays occasionally a light and agreeable facility for superficial
comedy, but his gleam is that of a gold-fish swimming
around in a whale's tank. He touches only the surfaces
of comedy; his characters are skin-deep; and he employs a tricky verbal adroitness to conceal his lack of
any real penetration of them. Now and then he gets
fairly close to one of his personages but soon thereafter sidles away timorously and takes refuge in badi-
nage to hide his own philosophical nervousness and
boyish uncertainty. When he tries drama of a more
sober nature as, for example, "Hotel Universe," he is
completely lost. What talent he has is for theatrical

May-pole dancing. Zoë Akins, who started out some years ago with genuine brilliance and who in "Papa" and "A Texas Nightingale" gave promise of a career of high achievement, seems to have blown up. Much of her later work, as has been observed often enough, is of affectation and posturing all compact, and has turned upon itself as burlesque. She periodically still shows momentary flashes of merit but they are seen to be only Summer lightning; her more recent plays have been simply an ingenuous whistling against thematic hurricanes, full of a modish trilling signifying nothing. The drama to her is just a Cecil De Mille gold bathtub. George S. Kaufman's top marks have been reached not singly but (1) in conjunction with Edna Ferber — their joint effort, "The Royal Family," being one of the best of American-made comedies; (2) in conjunction with Moss Hart — their "Once in a Lifetime" being as ironically humorous a farce as our stage has shown; and (3) in conjunction with Ring Lardner — the result being the highly droll "June Moon." Kaufman is certainly one of the more skilful and talented of the younger group of playwrights, though he seems to be able to do little without the aid of a collaborator. His "The Butter and Egg Man," written without a helper, is a fairly amusing topical farce-comedy but entirely unimportant. The plays he has written with Marc Connelly have contained isolated scenes of some humorous distinction but the plays as a whole belong in a minor category. The best of them, "Beggar on Horseback," owes its origin to Paul Apel's "Hans Sonnenstösser's Trip to Hell," upon which, despite the fact that the idea of an adaptation was kept carefully in the background, it leans heavily. Connelly, on his own, has turned out a weak little fantasy, "The Wisdom Tooth"; in collaboration with Herman Mankiewicz a dull comedy, "The Wild Man of Borneo"; and a generally excellent dramatization of Roark Bradford's southern Negro sketches under the title, "The Green Pastures." The credit for this play must obviously be shared. A word or two upon it.

The theatrical representation of God or His Direct Offspring has, in the modern drama, been confined either to a symbolical spotlight, the gutturals of a twenty-dollar-a-week actor stationed in the wings, or a member of the Actors' Equity Association with his face smeared with billiard chalk, and clad in an old Inverness coat. It remained for Connelly, with the considerable aid of Bradford, to get rid of such sacrilegious hocus-pocus and to introduce Him in person. The effect is so fine and so persuasive that the law which forbids the physical introduction of the Almighty into a play — ferociously yet ineffectually invoked by Mr. Morris Gest's press-agent when Mr. Gest anticipated sour business for his production of the Freiburg Passion Play at the Hippodrome — will doubtless be permitted to continue its slumbers.

There is irony in the circumstances that the God exhibited by the Messrs. Connelly and Bradford is at once revealed as a lowly Negro and as the most vividly impressive and lovably believable incarnation of the Deity that the stage has shown. Here is the Lord as He is seen through the imagination of the poor Southern Negroes: a cross between the kindly and respected parsons of their own humble churches and the preachers of the gospel in the somewhat grander churches just beyond the plantations. And here, for white as well as for black, are the substance and essence of godhood as all the spot-lights, chalk-faces, hollow voices and Inverness coats in earthly Christendom have never suggested and perhaps never could suggest them. The reason for this is, I believe, a simple one. Irony or no irony, it is a fact apparently unsuspected by the condescending critics who have fallen before the play's spell that most believers, black or white, ignorant or relatively intelligent, poor or rich, humble or powerful, socially ostracized or socially accepted, view the Almighty in much the same way. Save for a few details, quite negligible, there is very little difference between the visualization of the Lord by ignorant darkeys and by more educated whites. That is, taking class for class. The popular success of the Connelly-Bradford play and its picture of the Almighty goes a long way to prove this. For all the white audiences' pretence of superiority and theological *hauteur*, they are moved profoundly by this portrait of God and they believe in Him, nigger parson though his externals present Him. Their periodic laughter is a laughter not evoked by comedy but by sympathy, respect and love. Wash up the actor who plays the rôle, paint his face white and put him in a white nightgown instead of a rusty black Prince Albert, and the basic effect would be much the same from a psychical and religiously emotional, if not theatrical, point of view.

So great, indeed, was the impression made upon the white critics by "The Green Pastures" and its black God that they actually got religion and substituted a species of religious worship and even frenzy for cool and sober criticism. The idea of God, attributed to poor Southern Negroes, was obviously their own idea, modified but little, as it is the idea of most faithful whites. And the idea, being more powerful than the play into which it was injected and 'round which the play was built, took them like little children upon its knee and held them, as in childhood, to its breast. For belief with most men wears throughout life the kilts of boyhood; the God of the nursery and the God of later years are largely indistinguishable. Save in one point. As man grows up and achieves what he imagines to be increased intelligence, he paradoxically surrenders to God his childhood sense of criticism and takes Him wholeheartedly in all His virtues. But the child, like the Negro — who is the child eternal —

finds fault occasionally with God and sees Him as
occasionally human and erring. The white child ad-
dresses the Lord familiarly in his prayers as "dear
God"; he speaks to Him much in the language that he
speaks to his father; he tells Him what he wants for
Christmas, why he doesn't want it to rain on picnic day
as it did last year, how much he wants to be able to
lick the bully of the neighborhood, what happiness it
will give him to have a little baby brother to play
with, how sorry he is to have stolen the jam and been
found out, and how much more he will like Him if He
prevents his mother from spanking him. God is near
to him, and is a friend. It is only when he grows older
that God becomes more and more remote, more stern
and less loving. But the Negro, remaining a child,
speaks with God through all his life as he and the
white youngster have spoken with Him in childhood.

It is this God of the white child and the Negro that
moves upon the stage through the story of the Bible
as it is pictured by theoretically dumb black minds.
It is God not as we get Him in the utterances of Park
Avenue clergymen or in the tracts of New England
spinsters or in the tents of the evangelists. It is not the
God of complete wisdom, unbridled purity and comprehensive infallibility. It is God beautiful in His
humanity and wise beyond wisdom in His error. It is
God within human reach, within human understanding, within the human heart. The Throne of Biblical

frontispieces, lit up with gilt ink, has been cast into the rubbish heap and in its place there is a warm and cozy easy-chair and in that chair sits a Figure of real and living, rather than dim, remote and shadowy, grandeur.

The play itself, while often tender in its humor, quick with fancy and alive with invention, is nevertheless hardly the masterpiece the hypnotized critics have written it is. For all the strength and dominance of its central idea, its machinery runs out of oil periodically and disturbs one with its heavy whirring. And at times the author seems to dangle his sense of humor somewhat strainfully before him, like a three-sheet. In addition, the central idea is now and then rolled on the author's tongue with a bit too much obvious relish; one can discern his conscious pride in tasting its flavors. But, with all its flaws, the play's net effect is a curiously holding and curiously agitating one. It brings God down out of His heaven and closer to the hearts of men, white and black. And in it there is a ten times gentler and greater eloquence than in all the churches, Y.M. C.A.'s, Salvation Army camps and sawdust trails in the land.

Rachel Crothers, hailed fifteen years ago as one of the hopes of American drama, has written one or two pleasant little popular theatre pieces but, beyond that, has never given evidence that she is anything save a fairly adroit concocter of box-office stuffs. She is a hangover from the era of Thomas, Broadhurst, Sheldon and other such hollow pets of a hollow critical past. William Hurlbut has assiduously tried to tickle himself into a position of eminence with a Freudian feather but all that he has been able to achieve is a sensational squirming. He is a sophomoric Brieux, intent upon startling his audiences with blushful themes but without the talent to do other by them than to undress them in public. He writes too crudely and unimaginatively to dramatize his undertakings persuasively. Channing Pollock is simply a moralist turned playwright: he writes with one eye on the profitable endorsements of the clergy and with the other on the lucrative peasantry. His work is full of special pleading and is heavy with sentimentality.

Hatcher Hughes has written only one play that is worth even passing notice, "Hell-bent fer Heaven," and it is, for all its effort in an O'Neill direction, pretty feeble drama. His "Ruint" is cheap stuff and his "Wake Up, Jonathan," in collaboration with Elmer Rice, an exceptionally trivial comedy. Rice, who came to notice with "The Adding Machine," a pale copy of German Expressionism, begins with "Street Scene" to promise something. That play has moments of observation above the ordinary, though the substructure of the play itself is decidedly commonplace and though there is a disturbing injection of palpable hokum into what is otherwise often electric drama. Zona Gale has turned to the theatre from the novel, or rather with the novel, on two occasions. She remains a novelist; her acquaintance with dramaturgy is defective and her plays have the air of novels become talkies. Theatrical life is missing from them; they seem to call for reading lamps more than for actors. Bartlett Cormack has indicated more than merely melodramatic skill in his single play, "The Racket"; there are evidences in it of authentic character and of a sharp eye to life. What he will do in the future remains to be seen.

Booth Tarkington is no longer active as a playwright and, during the period of his activity, showed little more than a scent for lightly diverting comedy, notably in the piece called "Clarence." George Ade has left the theatre altogether after several comedies of very considerable merit. In Ade the American stage promised to discover its enormously superior Charley Hoyt but, after a brilliant start, Ade decamped and left the theatre flat. Frank Craven has written two comedies, "Too Many Cooks" and "The First Year," that rank well in the native comedy catalogue, but his more recent work shows a sharp decline and amounts to little. His wind, too, seems to have given out. Gilbert Emery, in "The Hero," presented tokens of talent, though since that play he has disclosed nothing to bring one seriously to consider his claims to potential celebrity. George Abbott and Philip Dunning seem to have shot their bolt with the journalistic melodrama "Broadway." Dunning has turned out only a couple of rubbishy melodramas since and Abbott has constituted himself a proficient tinkerer with other playwrights' box-office wares. Ben Hecht, who has an honest gift for the theatre, is, unless all signs fail, destined to position in the American playwriting circle. Even his earliest efforts, such as "The Egotist," showed a point of view and a humor rare in the local market. In Charles MacArthur he has found a valuable collaborator, a writer with an engagingly sardonic mind and a sense of broad humor that matches his own. These men form the most promising collaborative team presently in evidence. Their "The Front Page" shows the way their talents blow.

In "A Man's Man," Patrick Kearney managed a very fair job, but up to the moment he seems destined to be listed as a one-play playwright. In "Chicago," similarly, Maurine Watkins contrived the best farcical satire we have had, but nothing has come from her since. The two plays that she has written since "Chicago," which I have been privileged to read, contain few indications of sustained skill. Yet, even so, there is a peculiar quality hovering about them that, in some future manuscript, may come to flower. Owen Davis calls for little comment. Essaying late in his long career to turn his hand to the more reputable drama he has found that his portracted immersion in cheap box-office stuff has botched him, and all that he has been able to negotiate are vainglorious zeros. In "The Detour" and "Ice-bound" he tried to write O'Neill plays, but the ghosts of Bertha, Nellie and other such sweethearts of his playwriting past insinuated themselves into them and the results were grotesque. Rita Wellman did one estimable job some years ago in "The Gentile Wife," but has done nothing since that time. There were also moments of worth in Frederick Ballard's "Young America," produced years ago, but Ballard, like Miss Wellman, has shown nothing in the meantime. In Lula Vollmer, for all my colleagues' admiration, I can discover little. "Sun-Up" was fair in spots, but only fair. And none of her other attempts has come to anything.

Arthur Richman, in "Ambush," exhibited some dramatic talent and has since exhibited an even more substantial talent for light comedy. His work, however, even in the instance of a single manuscript, is disturbingly uneven; there are moments when he is excellent and moments, suddenly thereafter, when he descends to banality and doldrums. But there is wit to the fellow and he writes smoothly. Next to Vincent Lawrence, he is our neatest hand at what goes by the name of polite comedy. But both have some distance to go before they achieve fully sound work. Clare Kummer, after a couple of droll and original contributions, has retired from the theatre. While never an important playwright, she possessed a curious skill in the confection of comic

oddities and a mind piquantly alive to absurdity.
George M. Cohan's later plays miss all the originality
of his early ones; he impresses one as either laboriously retracing old ground or patterning his work after
certain other popular plays of the day. The racy Cohan
touch of fifteen years ago has disappeared. His work
is tired. Willard Mack, a theatrical Capone, has devoted himself to hoped-for money-makers, none of
them worth a continental. Samuel Shipman need not
be mentioned. Bayard Veiller is highly expert a
popular murder melodrama, but there his talent rests.
Robert E. Sherwood, in "The Road to Rome," proved
himself merely still another cuckooer of Shaw, and a
weak one. And his "The Queen's Husband" was little
more than college-boy satire, as his "Waterloo Bridge"
was simply a gummy rehash of the old prostitute-won-
to-purity theme. James Forbes has grown steadily
worse and worse; nothing he has delivered himself of
in recent years has been worth discussion. What fertil-
ity he exhibited in some of his early work has completely deserted him. Harry Wagstaff Gribble wrote
"March Hares," a very funny curio, but has done nothing since, although one or two passages in his "Revolt"
gave hint of his old originality and derisory humor.
Don Marquis contrived a good character in the Old
Soak and then incorporated it into a tenth-rate play.
His more serious attempts at drama have not been too
happy.

Lewis Beach occasionally touches the surfaces of authentic character but his aptitude for playwriting is so meagre that his labors come to naught. A. E. Thomas, though he writes well, has never come off as a playwright: his plays die of inanition before they have run half their course. The Nugents are simply elaborators of what should remain vaudeville sketches. The best of their efforts, "The Poor Nut," is feeble Ade crossed with Tarkington. Kenyon Nicholson has done little so far to argue for his future. Edward Childs Carpenter has written one amusing farce-comedy, "The Bachelor Father," but none of his other plays has been deserving of notice. Percy Mackaye began and ended with "The Scarecrow." And George Middleton, who has been writing plays, it seems, since before the time of man, has yet to produce anything worthy of critical attention.

Montague Glass, a first-rate delineator of character and a fine humorist, has collaborated upon several very amusing dramatizations of his stories and characters, but his theatrical vein appears to have run out. Louis Kaufman Anspacher is nowhere; his plays are utterly worthless. Fannie Hurst has given the stage only claptrap, and Mary Roberts Rinehart has offered nothing. Winchell Smith began and ended a box-office playwright, and Jules Eckert Goodman, save when he collaborated with Glass, showed himself a sorry figure in the business of playwriting. Earl Derr Biggers need not be discussed. Lee Wilson Dodd has amounted to nothing. Tom Barry, who years ago seemed to have something in him, has never realized his hintful promise. Thompson Buchanan appears to have exhausted himself long ago; the plays he has written in late years are gimcracks. James Gleason has written some amusing wisecracking dialogue, but his plays, whether his own or written in collaboration with others, are fundamentally trashy. Austin Strong is a fabricator of cheap theatrical valentines. John Emerson and Anita Loos have devoted themselves to negligible farces, the most adroit of which was their dramatization of Miss Loos' "Gentlemen Prefer Blondes."

Edward Sheldon, laid low by illness, has done little in later years and did little in the way of actual worth, rhapsodies to the contrary notwithstanding, in his heyday. Eugene Walter is heard of today only as a dallier with adaptations. Hubert Osborne need not be counted; his plays have been wholly unimportant. S. N. Behrman, however, takes rank as one of the country's promising writers of comedy. His "The Second Man" was an excellent job, and his "Meteor," though an inferior one, showed several traces of merit. Martin Flavin, whose "Children of the Moon" evoked an idiotic critical hymning, I can see nothing in. Edwin Justus Mayer has written a diverting minor comedy in "The Firebrand," and a graceful if undramatic play in "Children of Darkness." He has a gift for dialogue unsupported by an apt hand at dramaturgy. After "Goat Alley," an interesting study of the Negro, Ernest Howard Culbertson sank.

Jim Tully, in "Black Boy," showed a very real talent for drama but his virtues were corrupted by a hack collaborator. It will be interesting to see what he does when he undertakes playwriting on his own. The so-called New Playwrights group, John Howard Lawson, Em Jo Basshe, John Dos Passos, E. E. Cummings and Michael Gold, disclose nothing; they may be dismissed. Guy Bolton has devoted himself to commonplace box-office writing. Martin Brown has exuded only flapdoodle, and Porter Emerson Browne, save for an amusing but negligible comedy, "The Bad Man," has given the stage nothing worth talking about. David Carb has so far produced nothing save a commendable attempt at biographical drama, "Queen Victoria," in collaboration with Walter Prichard Eaton. Wilson Collison has delivered himself only of pornographic garbage. Barry Connors is a merchant of mush, and Milton Herbert Gropper of out-and-out balderdash. Catherine Chisholm Cushing isn't worth mentioning; Gladys Unger, a relic of past decades, has never written anything calling for notice; and Dan Totheroh has tried to shoot at the stars with a bean-blower. Lawrence Eyre has so far turned out only vacuums. William J. Rapp and Wallace Thurman may bear watching on the score of their work in "Harlem." The virtue of this play undoubtedly lies in the circumstance that it was written by a white man and a black man working in collaboration and that it accordingly avoids, on the one hand, that air of viewing the Negro as a curiosity under a microscope which attaches to most Negro plays and books written by white men and, on the other, that air of exhibiting the Negro as a misunderstood and overly estimable human being which attaches to most Negro plays and books written by black. The etiolated Mr. Rapp and the fuliginous Mr. Thurman have served as balance wheels one for the other, and their play, as a result, doubtless comes nearer to the truth of the particular set of Ethiops they deal with than it would have had it been written by either gentleman singly. The somewhat supercilious superiority, magnanimously and laboriously concealed, that the white Mr. Rapp might have been expected to show is thus counteracted by the somewhat undue sympathy for his race that might have been expected of the black Mr. Thurman and a sound average is struck, as it is similarly struck by other potential exaggerations on both sides operating against each other. What emerges is a play that is far from being one of marked quality but one that none the less has a great deal of accurate character observation, a considerable measure of authentic reflection of Negro conduct, and a pervasive feel of reality.

Although these attributes have not been lost upon

the more sagacious of the critical fraternity, the attitude of the latter toward the exhibit still reveals a share of the parrot notes of code criticism. One of these notes, as may be anticipated, is found in the complaint over the play's melodrama. Whenever an otherwise rational critic doesn't know what to say against a play whose defects he feels but is at a loss critically to get his fingers on, he invariably falls back upon the theory that it would have been a better piece of work if it weren't for its melodrama. He never, true enough, offers any good reason why it would have been better without its melodrama, but simply takes for granted that his readers, having been told nonsensically for years that melodrama is suspect, will arbitrarily catch his point and agree with him. I have yet to read a detraction of the melodrama in such a play as "Harlem" that argued that detraction intelligibly, yet never is such a play produced that the detraction isn't dished up with a kind of mechanical headwaiter disdain.

The melodrama of "Harlem," in point of fact, is completely relevant; it is part and parcel of the play and its characters; and it is as befitting and integral a part of the whole as the melodrama of the "Phoenissæ" of Euripides. The critics have become so many phonographs in the presence of melodrama. Any play that is labeled a melodrama, provided it deals with crooks and detectives, will get a pertinent and equitable appraisal. But any play that isn't called a melodrama and that contains, however congruously, certain melodramatic phases, will draw out of them a measure of doubt and misgiving. In all the history of modern drama, the only play that I can think of — not called a melodrama — that has had a pistol in it and has not been superiorly sniffed at for the fact is "Hedda Gabler."

Melodrama and the Negro are cut from the same cloth. The Negro's emotions have naturally all the exaggeration of melodrama; his imaginings, dreams, reactions to the world about him and even dress have all the high color of extravaganza and melodrama. This is true, I believe, of the educated Negro as well as of his nether brother, though to a lesser degree, of course. But it is true nevertheless. Read the books that he writes and you will find in them much of the basic indignation of melodrama. Read even his poetry and in much of it you will find the swollen emotion and defiance of melodrama. In Washington, D.C., there has recently been inaugurated an intellectual Little Negro Theatre movement. The plays for this theatre deal with Negroes and are written and acted by Negroes. I point to two of the first plays presented: "Compromise," by Willis Richardson, and "Chasm," by Mr. Richardson and E. C. Williams. The former is a melodrama in which a Negro compromises with a white man, who has killed his son, for one hundred dollars and drinks himself to death with the money.

His widow struggles to support her children. Her elder daughter is seduced by the son of the white man. Her son attacks the seducer and, in an attempt to kill him, severely wounds him. The white man swears vengeance against his boy's assailant but the latter escapes. The white man then turns to revenge himself on the mother who, as the final curtain falls, is loading a shotgun to let hell loose on the villain. The second play is a melodrama in which a Negro chauffeur has a love affair with a white girl, in which the girl's family, becoming privy to the news, raises the roof, and in which the girl stands at bay, finally defies them in a ringing address and melodramatically rushes out to join her black beau. The best of the more recent plays written by white men and dealing with the Negro — the fantasy, "The Green Pastures," alone excepted — have astutely appreciated the close relationship between the Negro and melodrama and have not hesitated to display the one in terms of the other; such plays, for example, as "Goat Alley," "Black Boy," "All God's Chillun Got Wings," "The Emperor Jones," "Porgy," *et al*.

Susan Glaspell has a talent far above that of the majority but her mastery of the dramatic form is weak and her plays, for all their fine intent, do not come off. They have a library smell that debilitates them. What she may do in the way of authentic drama is still problematical. Her mind, viewpoint and literary skill

are considerably above the average, however. Edward
Salisbury Field has a modest talent for trivial comedy
but without Margaret Mayo's collaboration has succeeded in doing nothing. Miss Mayo herself collapsed
long ago. Arthur Goodrich, Robert Housum and Edward Locke have disclosed no signs of anything; Max
Marcin is nil; and J. P. McEvoy, while not without
mild traces of ironic humor, revealed in "God Loves
Us," concerns himself chiefly with music shows. William Anthony McGuire is one of the box-office crowd;
Myron C. Fagan shows nothing; and Don Mullally
shows less. Roland Oliver is a tripe-seller. Fulton
Oursler has a good sense of plot and sometimes a point
of view removed from the commonplace, but his plays
are streaked through with immaturity. Samson Rapha-
elson has thus far produced only voids. Willard Robert-
son's plays are greasepaint *novilladas*. Lynn Starling
has some humor but his comedies are strained and
feeble. Anne Crawford Flexner has disappeared from
the scene. The Hattons are completely trashy.

John Wexley's "The Last Mile," based on another
writer's one-act play, has considerable melodramatic
quality; to appraise his talents more fully, one must
wait. Preston Sturges, with much help from his stage
producers and others, managed to turn out an amusing
light comedy in "Strictly Dishonorable," but in "Recapture," a sample of his solo effort, he revealed himself in a poor light. Hugh Stange wrote a fair tragi-

comedy in "Veneer," but his other plays to date have been wholly negligible, and Lynn Riggs has still to prove his minnesinger mettle. Ring Lardner, an admirable humorist, has written a very comical farce, "June Moon," with the help of George S. Kaufman, but the plays which he has contrived single-handed have been dramaturgically defective. Lardner is generally praised for his gift of recording the common speech with a jocose exactness. But in the praise there is often overlooked his even greater talent, to wit, the quick stamping of character by means of a discriminating analysis of the content of such speech as the particular character would think in it and use it. It is a talent that even George Ade never possessed in his slang day, for Ade's characters' speech issued from their mouths rather than, as in Lardner's case, from their intrinsic natures. There is hardly a character in "June Moon," for instance, that doesn't become immediately recognizable for what he afterwards fully proves himself to be the moment he opens his lips and says his first say. In his plays as in his stories, Lardner pictures character not so much by act as by speech, not so much by physical identification as by verbal. And I am not certain, for all the critical eloquence often issued to the contrary and for all that is written about introspection, psychical development and incisive external description, that this is not at times a pretty good method.

"As a man thinketh, so is he in his heart" may be true enough, but as a man outwardly speaketh, so is he, also, in his essential nature, even when he happens to be something of a fraud and faker. The character of the man who said, "We are never more true to ourselves than when we are inconsistent" and "Misfortunes one can endure, they come from outside, they are accidents; but to suffer for one's faults — ah! there is the sting of life" — the character of such a man is thereby as quickly to be appraised as from Sherard's, Harris' or any other such elaborate study of him. The character of the poet who on his deathbed said, "Lift me up, Horace, I want to so-and-so," flashes back into a composite picture of his earthly mind, attitude and psyche. We often recognize, know, understand and remember men from so little as a single typical and illuminating expression. "Après moi, le déluge!", "My only regret is that I have but one life to give to my country," "God is on the side of the strongest artillery," "Was für Plünderung!", "The public be damned," "Let him who is without sin cast the first stone" and "She hit me first" each provides a more eloquent analysis of its spokesman's character than any ten thousand words of description that might be written of him. "You know me, Al," is a snapshot of a man revelatory of his nature, character and very look. As you hear Lardner's dialogue you promptly recognize and know intimately, even with your eyes closed, the men who speak it. You can see their faces, their clothes, their each future act, their very gizzards. The common notion that Lardner is simply a flash-tongue phonograph is silliness glorified. He is a sharp observer and creator of character who masks his high proficiency in that greatest misgiving and hobgoblin of professorial criticism: low humor.

There are certain other playwriters whose names I have omitted who may some day do something to surprise us, but of that happy surprise they have not as yet given us any vividly perceptible omens.

§ 2

*The English Comedy Writers.*— One of the reasons why the English and Irish-English playwrights generally write better comedies than the American lies in the fact that so many of them are at bottom tragic, or at least serious, dramatists and in the further and obvious related fact that the best comedy is simply tragedy in falseface. A very considerable number of them have actually begun as writers of tragedy, problem plays or some other species of serious drama — or as serious novelists — and subsequently have come to look at the world with a less gray and more critically humorous eye. Down in the heart of every American writer of comedy there crawls a desire for the more serious drama; to him it seems a step forward in importance. But down in the heart of the English and Irish-English writers of serious plays there crawls an antithetical desire for comedy; to them it means a step forward in worldly wisdom and philosophical development. In which, as always, we have the mark of an older and more fully flowered civilization and culture.

Take a few examples. Galsworthy began in the vein of "The Silver Box," "Strife" and "Justice" and that vein produced the bloom of comedy in "The Pigeon." Drinkwater came into his comedy own with "Bird in Hand" after a long apprenticeship in the sober chronicle drama. Even the mocking Shaw, until lately a genius of comedy, began in the relatively indignant mood of "Widowers' Houses" and "Mrs. Warren's Profession." Maugham's earliest efforts were of "A Man of Honor" flavor and Macdonald Hastings' of "The New Sin." Arnold Bennett's "What the Public Wants" was the forerunner of his several amusing comedies and Lennox Robinson's hilarious "The White-headed Boy" followed a period of dramatic acidity. "The Wife Without a Smile" and other such excellent comedies are the work of the same man who wrote "The Second Mrs. Tanqueray," "The Notorious Mrs. Ebbsmith" and "Iris." "The Tyranny of Tears" and "The Saving Grace" are the comedies of the author of such antecedent problem drama as "John-a-Dreams." The comedies of H. V. Esmond were preceded by things like "Grierson's Way." The comedies called "The Case of Rebellious Susan," "The Liars" and "Joseph Entangled" are the products of the same playwright who wrote "Judah," "Michael and His Lost Angel" and "Mrs. Dane's Defence." Maugham, already referred to, the author of a number of admirable comedies, is also the author of "The Moon and Sixpence" and "Of Human Bondage." And St. John Ervine, author of the comedy, "The First Mrs. Fraser," is the same tragic-minded Ervine who began with "Mixed Marriage," "Jane Clegg" and "John Ferguson." I do not say, plainly enough, that comedy is the sole end of these Englishmen and Irish-Englishmen, for in some cases they have periodically returned to serious drama after gratifying themselves in comedy. What I do say is that their comedies are what they are because they are the slow outgrowth of minds with serious roots.

§ 3

*The French Undramaticists.*— A movement seems to be under way in France to rid the drama of drama. It appears to be the enthusiastic purpose of a considerable portion of contemporary French authors to concoct plays with the least possible amount of theatrical stimulation. Drama, in the usual sense, is evidently regarded by them as peculiarly obnoxious and they exert themselves to the limit to write plays that shall sedulously avoid it. They may be called the undramatic school of dramatists and their credo may be defined as a denial of action and an affirmation of inertion. Shaw said of Sardou that his plan of playwriting was first to invent the action of his piece and then carefully to keep it off the stage and have it announced merely by letters and telegrams. The characters, he observed, open the letters and read them, whether they are addressed to them or not, and then talk either about what the letters announce as having occurred already or about what they intend to do tomorrow in consequence of receiving them. These grandchildren of Sardou have got rid of even the letters and telegrams.

In this dramaless school of dramatists we find such men as Paul Raynal, Jean-Jacques Bernard, Charles Vildrac and the later Louis Verneuil. Of Bernard's theatrical "stills," and of Vildrac's, I have written in the past. Samples of Raynal's and Verneuil's may come in for a little further consideration. The former's "Le Tombeau Sous l'Arc de Triomphe" and the latter's "Monsieur Lambertier" exemplify nicely the lengths to which the academy of Bernard *et Cie* arbitrarily goes to substitute inaction for movement and beefy reflection for nervous thought, movement and speech. Verneuil is the lesser offender of the two; there are moments when drama, for all his tugging and pulling against it, creeps into his manuscript like a rebellious ghost out of his playwriting past. But, obedient to the preposterous new dispensation, he quickly gets it by the sheet-tail and exorcizes it. To make doubly sure that there shall be a minimum of drama in his exhibit, he manages, after much obvious sweat, to fashion it with only two characters, as Raynal, by dint of equally obvious effort, manages to fashion his with only three. Both plays clearly demand a fuller set of characters; both plays would be infinitely better with a greater number; both literally bawl for the entrance of characters arbitrarily kept in the wings. Yet the authors, intent upon detheatricalization, puff and groan self-consciously and absurdly in keeping them in exile and in a consequent reduction of assertion to implication and of alert drama to rhetoric. So far in this direction does Raynal's play go that it resembles that part of a moving picture that has been left in the cutting-room. It is as if the play we see were a patchwork of all the undramatic portions cut out of an originally dramatic play and pieced together.

This attempt to confect a drama that shall impress and move a theatre audience by inferential rather than by more direct means is, I daresay, but another aspect of the prevailing auctorial desire to achieve facile notice by a figurative brushing of the hair with a tooth-brush. We have thus been entertained by the spectacle of a troupe of charlatans writing six character plays in terms of two or three, keeping their central characters off-stage and hidden from view, presenting synopses of plays in the guise of plays, substituting trick scenery for able dramaturgy, Expressionisming and Impressionisming themes that, if they knew how to write plays, were more soundly to be treated with the very much more difficult and evasive standard technique, and otherwise seeking to convince the world that they are revolutionary generals when it is plain to see that what they really are are simply so many *sans-culottes* with popguns.

The theatre, after all, is the theatre, and audiences of even the highest intelligence do not go to it to avoid drama. To ask such audiences to be impressed and moved by the mere externals of drama is like trying to impress and move a reader by hitting him on the head with a book. A two and one-half hours' two-character exhibition like "Monsieur Lambertier" might conceivably be converted into drama by a genius, but in the hands of an average playwright it is drama only occasionally and for the most part merely a shadow and hint of drama. In the same way, a two and one-half hours' three-character affair like "Le Tombeau Sous l'Arc de Triomphe" becomes, under the pen of an inferior playwright, simply excessive garrulity that cries loudly for the relieving commas and dashes of a modicum of visualized action. For action in the common theatrical sense, I have as little use as the next man, but for two and one-half hours of talk between a couple of actors I must say that I have even less. If I crave that sort of pastime, I'd much rather call up some intelligent and amusing friend and let him talk my head off. It is all very well to say that a dramatist may be able to deliver himself, through a pair or a trio of actors, of several hours of ripping good dramatic colloquy, but unfortunately for the facts there has never been a dramatist who was able to do so. Even Shaw, one of the best talkers living and a playwright who would rather talk than eat, has never made the mistake of trying the trick. The talkiest of his plays, such as "Misalliance" and "Getting Married," have a stageful of characters to divert an audience and, in the very thick of their discourse, are careful to coddle the audience's additional interest by theatrical or dramatic shenanigan of one kind or another. There have been some good plays with only two characters, but they have been one-act plays and have run for only about twenty or twenty-five minutes. There have been good longer plays that really needed only two characters, but it has taken the shrewdness of a Strindberg, who wrote one of the best of them ("Fröken Julie"), to hold an audience's attention by condensing his original three-act manuscript into a single act.

These Frenchmen are not sincere in their dramaturgy. They are not intent upon writing sound drama; they are rather simply eager to show off as dramatic parlor magicians. They are less dramatists than stage prestidigitators masquerading as dramatists. If a play contains an important character and its subject matter calls for his presence, an audience has a right to see that character, save perhaps he be God Almighty or Christ in a piece of religious claptrap, under which circumstances certain concessions to theological punctilio and to the modesty of even an actor may be allowed. If a play and its theme contain the germs of vital action, an audience has a right to that action and it may not be airily philosophized into the wings with tea-table chatter. The Frenchmen's dodges may be all very well for the novel, but in the theatre they are self-defeating and bogus. The novel may simply tell the reader something; the stage must not only tell the spectator, it must also show him.

§ 4

*The German Romantics.*— Alfred Neumann, with Bruno Frank, Max Brod, Oskar Maria Graf, Frank Thiess and Fritz von Unruh, is one of the figures in the German literary troupe which has come into conspicuous notice since the outbreak of the late war. His novel, "The Devil," has made him a much discussed personage not only in the malty halls of Herr Horcher, but far across the somewhat drier borders. As in the instance of his colleagues Frank and von Unruh, though less than the last named, the theatre tickles his fancy, and that tickle has taken the form of a play called "The Patriot." With some of von Unruh's plays, I presume you are familiar. During the war, he turned out at least one that, because of its bass-drum and bugle racket over militarism, worked its way into the cable dispatches, and another, "Bonaparte," has been published here in an English translation. A third, an attempt at satire of the cinema, has lately been on view in Berlin. Frank's play, "Twelve Thousand," a tale of the mercenaries in the American War of the Revolution seen through German eyes, and in my opinion the best of the lot, has already had an American performance.

"The Patriot" reaches the English-speaking countries in a shipshape translation by Ashley Dukes. This Dukes, as any of you who know his comedy, "The Man with a Load of Mischief," are aware, handles the King's tongue with an uncommon facility and grace, and in the present instance, with all due apologies to Neumann, he has actually succeeded in periodically giving the German author's work a measure of the air that it does not quite achieve in the original. That work seeks to reconstruct the scene in Petersburg in 1801, with its conspiracy against the violent weakling, Paul I, that led to his assassination and the placing upon the Czarist throne of Alexander, his son. The enterprise makes for fairish drama of venerable cut and from it emerges, in the character of Pahlen, Governor of Petersburg and the confederacy's brains, a portrait alive and pumping with grease-paint blood. It is in the picture of this Pahlen that Neumann, as the French say, earns his theatrical beefsteak. As a dramatic rôle, it is constituted of the sort of stuff that must make poor Mansfield roll around enviously in his grave, but — more important — as a suave and sure piece of hokum writing it so lifts itself above the rest of the manuscript that all that one remembers of the latter, once its leaves and its stage course are turned, are the march of soldiers' feet below the windows and a couple of pistol shots.

That manuscript, despite or perhaps because of its surface theatrical effectiveness, recalcitrantly suggests our venerable friend, Sardou, though Neumann writes so much better than the late lamented that the comparison may justifiably be a bit odious to him. Yet the ghost of "Diplomacy" lighted by the candelabra of "Tosca" and "Fedora" discernibly moseys in and out of the play, and once off-stage lingers in the wings discharging *sotto voce* grunts and gurgles. The Baroness Ostermann, as Neumann gives her to us, steps directly out of the defunct Victorien's pages; Pahlen himself, in certain of his stage manifestations, has surely acted in at least one Sardou play; and there are instances of stage business that the French dramatist would have little difficulty in recognizing. It is to Neumann's credit that he is able to throw his customers partly off the scent by some wily dramatic writing, but that scent remains none the less sufficiently odoriferous. I expose a few of its typical perfumes. Thus, Pahlen to the plotting Baroness: "Remember, Anna, there is no hope of worming your way into my secrets! Affairs of state for me, affairs of the heart for you; is that agreed?" Thus, the Baronness, in Neumann's own words "recoiling": "I should defend myself with every weapon, Peter — yes, with all your wits and all my instinct. I should drag you down to the dust, Peter, and then I would gladly begin to climb again with you, step by step, if our limbs were still unbroken." (Shades of Sardou? Shades of Charles Garvice!) Thus, further, such phrases and lines as "those fierce eyes of yours"; "the net is spread"; "You staked our fortunes together on one throw"; "My dear Pahlen, since when have your footmen shown me in and out of your presence?"; "I will not flatter you by suspecting a woman in the case"; "Do you know what you are saying, Baroness? Have you forgotten that in this country a thoughtless word may cost a life?"; and "Surely you will not turn me out into the snow" — all appearing in the *first two minutes* after the first curtain goes up. Thus, still further, Pahlen: "One moment, Ivan! The Baroness must know nothing of this visitor. She will not leave her room while he is in the house, and not a word will be said of our interview. Now, my man, can I depend on you?" And thus — for there is surely no need to shadow the jury longer — "There are spies everywhere — yes, even round the Governor's house!"; "In these mistrustful days, I should have thought concealment —"; "Before you retired, you made sure that I was carrying papers on me"; "Do you mean that you put that paper into my hands for some motive of your own?"; "Take care, Count, take care! I may still be a match for you, if it comes to that! That paper in your hand betrays your conspiracy against the Czar!"; and — lovely solo for the organochordium, and exit — "I secure your silence, my dear Baroness, in a way that is least painful to you — by making you one of the conspirators! You will oblige me first of all by taking a sheet of writing paper with your monogram upon it — yes, so. And now you will write me the most affectionate letter you can manage to compose. A few lines will do. You will oblige me by losing no time. Write!" *Ære perennius!*

Neumann, it is plain, is of a romantical disposition toward the theatre. Frank shows a like attitude, though with none of Neumann's often spurious grease-paint, for Frank writes for the stage with his eyes and ears closed to strutting actors, pipe-organ speeches and so-called "effective" theatre. And, as a consequence, his work's persuasiveness steams up from its almost naïve simplicity. Both men, but Neumann in particular, are all too evidently secessionists from the German dramatic school, various as it is, that has apotheosized

realism and made the Teutonic stage on occasion indistinguishable from a vivisection clinic. Just before
the war and in the early stages of the rumpus, there
sprang up in the Fatherland a group of young playwrights, many of them without previous dramatic experience, who, in their own minds, were determined to
tell The Truth about everything from militarism to sex
and from sex to theology and *Kalbsragout*, or be good
and damned in the attempt. One wing, taking its cue
from Wedekind, posed itself against the sexual Rotari-
anism of the theatre and began writing plays in which
the libido was stripped of its pantaloons and made to
perform through astonishing and often excessively
recherché hoops. Another, taking its cue in turn from
Kaiser, proceeded to kick out the drama of established
form and to confect plays skeletonized down to the
last realistic knuckle, setting forth in terms of Expressionism and Impressionism themes previously reserved
for insane asylums and the novels of Hanns Heinz
Ewers. Still another went about making monkey-noses
at the military drama of the Halbe, Dinter and Beyer-
lein tradition and in manufacturing plays that re-
sembled slaughter-houses with the animals in Prussian
regimentals. Everywhere, the passion for hypothetical
realism and for sensationalism was apparent, until the
German stages and the German play publishers' lists
began in combination to take on the aspect of a psycho-
analytical and cinematic chowder party. But the wind

seems now to be turning; the German drama begins to show signs of returning to a romantic key. The writing of plays in which all the characters were horribly killed off by smallpox germs inserted into their *Setz-eier Meyerbeer* by the evil Hohenzollerns, a theme favorite of all indignant young Socialists and Republicans who had contracted cooties and enemy gonococci during the war, has seemingly ceased, as has also the writing of plays in which various Otto Emil Œdipuses became intimately Greek with as many Tilly Jocastas. Slowly there appears to be coming back into the German drama the more or less beery note. Its sound is perhaps not yet altogether clear and distinct, but the ear catches its faint tone none the less.

Neumann and Frank, among others, are, as I have observed, parties to the new movement, the former being a throw-back to the early '80's, the latter — in a company apart — being what may be described as a romantic realist. Neumann's "The Patriot" has been received so hospitably by his own people that one may believe they are ready for a turtle-turn in their dramatic fare and are tired of the old Jack-the-Ripper stage stuff. The play, as I have noted, has utterly no value or significance as drama, though it has a certain significance in showing the altered tendency of dramatists and theatre audiences in the land of its origin. It will not be long, I predict, before Germany will be swept by revivals of the romantic plays of the last century. "The Patriot" itself is, after all, little more than such a revival.

§ 5.

*The Spanish Writers.*— Whenever such a play as the Quinteros' "El Centenario" is produced in America and fails to make much of an impression, there is a critical disposition to attribute its failure (*a*) to the local unfamiliarity with and hence disinterest in Spanish provincial types, (*b*) to the placid uneventfulness of its dramaturgy, and (*c*) to the too great calm implicit in its theme. That the failure is due rather and simply to the fact that it is a very bad play does not seem to occur to those who choose to make a difficult problem out of something as plain as the noses on their faces. The truth about much of present-day Spanish drama is that it is so greatly underwritten that it is hardly drama at all, but merely drama struggling for birth in its own womb. This underwriting is accepted in certain critical quarters as a virtue founded upon deliberate artistic reticence, when what it actually is founded upon is imaginative impotence and dramaturgical ineptitude. A play like the one mentioned fails to warm its auditor not because of its unfamiliar personages, its placidity or its supine theme but because its authors do not know how to lay hold of its materials and inject a dramatic life, however moderate, into them.

Martinez Sierra, among modern Spanish playwrights, most closely resembles the Quintero brothers
in approach, manner and technique of writing but,
though his plays, like theirs, are lacking in what we
call action, they nevertheless contain a sufficient measure of theatrical glow to create something of a stir out
front. They are not sound plays any more than the
Quinteros' are, but the writing in them, unlike the lat-
ters', is often — apart from considerations of theatrical drama — lifting on its own account and so from
time to time catches the attention of the reader-mind
in the audience even when the dramatic-mind is left
unsatisfied. Each critical objection to the Quinteros'
plays may be lodged with equal exactness against
"Cradle Song" or "The Kingdom of God," yet such
plays of Sierra, as audiences have proven, exercise an
effect that the Quinteros' plays do not. The Quinteros
are cold writers; their plays, whether good or bad,
remain cold. Sierra's is a warmer pen; his plays,
whether good or bad in turn, have some degree of
heat.

Criticism, as I have hinted, has a way of walking all
around the block in such cases in order to get to the
house next door. It searches pedantically for reasons
that do not figure in the argument and that are brought
forth just to make things look a little harder. The
antic is always observable when a play from the south

of Europe happens along, for there seems to be something about the Latin drama, however negligible, that makes critics believe it calls upon their more punditical faculties and demands of them an unwonted sobriety. Three times out of four it does so no more than the Broadway drama or the Piccadilly drama, yet the critical nonsense persists. Quite as many bad plays are written in Spain and Italy as are written in New York and Chicago, but it will be some years before our theatrical commentators persuade themselves to digest the news. The reasons cited by the critics for the failure of the Quintero plays are not reasons at all; their hollowness may readily be appreciated by assigning them, with equal relevance, to plays that have succeeded. If, for example, local unfamiliarity with and hence disinterest in certain remote and alien types are responsible for the failure of such a play as "El Centenario," a like local unfamiliarity with and theoretical disinterest in Silesian peasants have somehow not caused the plays of Hauptmann to be failures. If, for further example, the failure of the Quinteros' plays is to be ascribed to the placid uneventfulness of their dramaturgy, the success of some such play as Davies' "The Mollusc" must be explained paradoxically in the same way. And if, in still further example, the Spanish plays fail because of the too great calm implicit in their themes, Barrie's "Alice-Sit-by-the-Fire" should surely fail on the same grounds.

§ 6

*Dramatists of War.*— For a reason that I have never been able to make out, there seems to be a general critical belief that a great war should subsequently give birth to great war plays. The simple fact that, since the time of the Greeks, no war has ever immediately inspired and produced a great war play appears to be lost upon the critics. Doubtless basing their conviction upon the theory that fine emotional drama should promptly flower from high emotion experienced and suffered and upon the collateral theory that war, as no other human enterprise, offers opportunity for such experience and suffering, they continue to argue theory grounded upon theory in the face of disturbingly opposing fact.

Why a great war should not give sudden birth to a great war play, I do not know. There doesn't seem to be any good reason why it should not. If such minor catastrophes as a single man's death have provided the material for great tragedy, why should not the death of tens of thousands of men provide the material for tragedy even greater? As I say, I do not know. Yet the truth seems to be that, since centuries before the birth of Christ, war has never immediately converted itself into fine emotional dramatic literature. Æschylus, himself a warrior, having written the "Persians," with its notable description of the battle of Salamis, is perhaps the father of the enduring critical faith, a faith that persists, even in the consideration of the classics, in overlooking the farcical satire visited upon the emotions of war by the ribald Aristophanes. Great war and great emotional war drama, for more than two thousand years, have not gone hand in hand. Long time must pass until genius, born centuries later, may look backward upon legend and history and in rare instance convert that look into proud drama. And such genius seldom itself is found to have worn a sword or carried a gun.

Of the large number of plays born directly out of the late war and dealing directly with it — Werfel's "Goat Song" does not come within that classification — only two may be said to merit discussion on the point of even relative quality, yet two, at that, is a high average considering the statistics since the years of Themistocles and Miltiades. The two are the American Anderson's and Stallings' "What Price Glory?" and the British Sherriff's "Journey's End," the former infinitely better than the latter. France has produced nothing. Its high-water mark, Raynal's "Le Tombeau Sous l'Arc de Triomphe," is an unsuccessful attempt to conceal a superior indignation in inferior dramatic prosody. For the rest, the Gallic war drama has consisted entirely in spectacles showing us the emotional disturbances of loyal French women married to Alsatians of dubious patriotism, the melodrama incidental to the unmasking of spies and the agony incidental to the loss of female chastity at the hands of German lieutenants. Italy, Austria, and Belgium have been completely sterile. Germany has turned out little save violent tracts against militarism, a considerable proportion of them couched in the Expressionistic madness, and various odds and ends deploring the capitalistic and monarchical impulses behind slaughter. England has produced, aside from Galsworthy's "The Mob," which does not fall into the direct category under discussion, nothing but Sherriff's play, and the United States nothing but Anderson's and Stallings'. The rest, in both countries, has been in the main little more than the kind of stuff retrospectively evoked, in Europe, by the Franco-Prussian war and, in America, by the Civil — that is, the banal triangle drama with uniforms substituted for evening dress and a pounding upon bass-drums for the clatter of tea cups, with now and then the addition of some such climactic melodramatic rubbish as the dash of a cavalry horse across the stage or the swinging of the heroine on the tongue of a bell.

From this counterfeit emotionalism, both "What Price Glory?" and "Journey's End" emerge as oddities. Neither comes, of course, under the head of fine drama of which we have been speaking, but both are superior to all the other plays of the war. Of the twain, as I have observed, "What Price Glory?" gets

the palm. A diagnosis of the reasons for the award need
not be entered into here; I have already in an earlier
book reviewed the merits of the American play at
length. The relative status of the two exhibits may be
appreciated, however, from a present consideration of
the English work. That work, the first play written by
its author and originally designed as a vehicle for the
talents of a group of amateurs, deals with the influence
of war upon a number of English civilians, now officers
in a dugout in the British trench before St. Quentin in
the March of 1918. Its virtues, which are several, lie
in the periodic sound and logical evocation of emotion
proceeding from character closely observed and
simply transcribed, in the general avoidance of the
fault of most plays dealing with war, to wit, over-
dramatization, and in the occasional adroit development of character in terms of ever-sensed, ever-felt and
ever-heard but still more or less shadowy external
forces. The war hovers over Sherriff's manuscript like
a child's inarticulate dread of the dark; it lays hold
of his personages with a ghostly hand; it insinuates itself into the chambers of their hearts, minds and souls;
but, though they laugh it off or cower before it, it comes
down upon them from without and makes them its own.
It is the undertone, in a word, that drowns out the overtones of antecedent character.

So much Sherriff has contrived and contrived well.
But at many moments when his writing is about to

reach its highest point of allectation and conviction, he vitiates his work by the injection into it of
cheap theatrical fetches. I call attention, for example,
to such obvious slices of hokum as the introduction of
a Cockney out of a Harry Tate vaudeville sketch, with
his wheezes about soup, to relieve dramatic tension;
as the scene in which men in the face of impending
danger affect a strainful unconcern and even nonchalance; as the hero's elaborate pretence of merri-
ment to conceal a breaking heart, or the equivalent
thereof; as the nostalgic meditations on England in the
Springtime; as the heavy jokes about bad cooking, including the one about the biscuit that one has to break
by hitting it against a chair; and as the scene out of
a score of tinpot melodramas in which an audience
startle is negotiated for in the business of having a
man with a revolver confront another man and of having him slowly count the seconds before he announces
that he will shoot. These are patently the devices of the
mob theatre; they are hardly those of authentic and
estimable drama.

Another element that works somewhat humorously
against the honesty of Sherriff's play is the over-
stressed and slightly offensive implication of the stu-
pendous heroism and gentlemanliness of Englishmen
in the mass. Sherriff's characters are clearly set forth
not as isolated specimens but as symbols of the general, and his admiration and respect for the superior

qualities of his fellow countrymen are embodied in the various types that he offers. Now, while I personally share some of his admiration and respect for some Englishmen, I experience considerable difficulty in accepting his comprehensive valuation as he asks me to. Englishmen are surely not always and invariably the heroic and gentlemanly creatures that he elects to have us believe, any more than Germans, Frenchmen, Italians, Liberians or Americans are. Yet Sherriff's Englishmen, even to his English coward who changes his colors under the fine indignation of another Englishman and who goes into battle and to possible death under the stern nobility of English ordered duty, are not only the salt of soldiery but gentlemen *de luxe* among gentlemen.

With all the esteem in the world for Englishmen — well, I don't believe it. I don't believe that eight or nine Englishmen such as Sherriff shows us gathered together in a dugout in France would have comported themselves as Sherriff requests us to imagine they would or did. I may be wrong but, though I appreciate that when an American gets drunk he talks wistfully about his dear little wife and when an Englishman does he talks wistfully about the primroses blooming back home in the April gardens, I still doubt that, drunk or sober and with the Hun less than a hundred yards away, Englishmen at St. Quentin delivered themselves of such tender meditations out of the worst of the early

Horace Annesley Vachell plays. Nor can I persuade myself, with all the good will and respect in the world, to imagine a group of British soldiers, some of them already more than three years in the filth and fury of war, carefully refraining from even a trace of high profanity, conducting the bulk of their speech much after the punctilio of Pinero actors, treating the dugout in the light of a gentleman's club, disgustedly objecting to allusions to loose women, and condescending to masculinity in the rough only in desultory and somewhat abashed references to whiskey, cockroaches and French post-cards. Finally, may I add a bit of skepticism that men — whether English, American or what not — are generally in the habit of facing death, be they heroes or just ordinary soldiers, with such indifferent and carefree *prosits* as "Cheero" or "Righto."

Where "Journey's End" lifts itself above the bulk of the war plays and above its own effeminate and even androgynous shortcomings is in its occasional scenes of honest emotion dredged up out of character unsentimentalized and momentarily caught for what it honestly is, in its periodic strainlessness and dramatic ease, and in its skilful suggestion of external psychic forces operating upon its personages.

It begins to look as if the dawn of a new dramatic approach to war were with us. Apparently done is the day of the play that presents war to us in terms of speech indistinguishable from the pencilings on the walls of an Elks' lavatory, or as a romantic *passage* with a French rural cutie orchestrated with the distant bursting of bombs and the detonation of bass-drums, or as a spectacle in which the fate of democracy hangs upon the star actress' ferocious preservation of her hymen, or as one in which the hero, rather than let the plans of the Allied advance fall into the enemy's hands, chews the papers into a *pâté* and swallows them.

§ 7

*Rolland.*—— Playwrights like Romain Rolland take for the skeletons of their plays the stalest of greasepaint plots and seek to distract attention from their antiquity by embroidering them with the species of writing that is called literary by such critics as imagine that when a man of letters fails to write dramatic dialogue what he has written must, by an arbitrary process of elimination, inevitably be literature. Rolland writes neither drama nor literature, but only a pretentious imitation of both.

§ 8

*Shaw.*—— In the last half dozen years it has become increasingly and regrettably obvious that, despite a chaste life, the digestion of tons of peas, spinach and string beans, and undoubted genius, the late sixties of his days brought with them the collapse of the high and engaging talents of Mr. George Bernard Shaw. In the sad fact we have perhaps less a criticism of Mr. Shaw than of his Maker, for the latter so often has a cruel way of killing His older artists' gifts before he kills their bodies. But, wherever the blame may rest, the melancholy news remains. The onetime sharpness of mind, so brilliantly exhibited in some of the best prefaces ever embalmed in printer's ink, has seen its edges dulled in a platitudinous treatise on capitalism and socialism, dedicated — to their understandable irritation — to intelligent women. The wit that once had the sparkle of champagne has now only the sparkle of soda pop, and exhausts its fizz in newspaper supplement articles on the talkies and in colloquies with American cowboy music-show comedians and prize-fighters who have achieved a reading of the novels of Thornton Wilder and have discovered to their pleasurable surprise that one of Shakespeare's characters is a wrestler. And the dramatist of a number of modern classics rich in beautiful irony, in thoughtful comedy, in insight, tenderness and a general prophylaxis now, in "The Apple Cart," reveals himself to be a repetitious, often banal and quite tiresome old man.

This "Apple Cart" is a bit of sardonic rosemary laid left-handedly by its author on his own grave. For all the shrewd showmanship that has gone into its manufacture — and Shaw's showmanship is the only thing about him that shows no trace of age —, for all the shrewdly planned assaults upon the applause-machinery of his admirers, for all the faint echoes of the often still winning bumptiousness, and even for all the scattered tokens of die-hard humorous penetration, there is about it something of the air of the death-chamber, peopled by the occasionally gay ghosts of yesterday's genius but damp, depressing and infinitely pathetic withal. Even when these ghosts disport themselves in the manner they were wont to before their whiskers had completely whitened and when, in the masquerade of Caesars and Napoleons and Brass-bounds and Tanners, they turned the stage topsy-turvy, they still remain mere ghosts — ghosts of the old Shavian wit, the old Shavian philosophical exercises, the old Shavian insolence and giddy bounce. One can only too plainly discern the effort it takes Shaw to make them and their opinions stand on their heads without falling over. One can only too plainly discern the weakness of the old strings that, so long used, must now be gingerly handled lest they break in the puppet dance.

There are, as has been observed, a few moments in the play when the sage of Whitehall Court is the gala fellow he once was. There is the speech of King Magnus in the first act, for example, in which a touch of the old Shavian dialectic and paradoxical wisdom and

humor peeks once more out of the past. And there is
the speech of the King again at the conclusion of the
play in which, with much of Shaw's old dexterity, he
puts his enemies to rout. But what goes between is
painfully forced and transparently tired thinking and
writing. And even more painfully forced and even
more tired humor. When the American ambassador
announces to the king that the United States has torn
up the Declaration of Independence and again seeks
coalition with the British Empire, the stage is all set for
the Shaw of yesterday and for a circus of the old
Shavian jocosities. But what do we get? We get nothing
but an actor giving a pale imitation of Sinclair Lewis'
Babbitt, along with a dull recitation of the wheezes of
Booth Tarkington's and Harry Leon Wilson's Man
from Home, and of such further barber-shop weekly
animadversions as the surplusage of Americans in
Paris, the removal of Queen Anne bedrooms to Pas-
saic, New Jersey, and the American's indefatigable
habit of shaking hands. The grand joke is posed, but
what follows the posing is the seediest kind of refurbished vaudeville sidewalk conversation. Consider,
too, the middle section of the play, the scene played
by the King and his platonic mistress in the latter's
boudoir. The degree of perspicacity here consists
largely in the already familiar news that a man often
deserts his wife for a much less worthy and attractive
woman, and the humor in a weary repetition of the

rolling-on-the-floor monkey-business that the playwright employed in "Great Catherine."

The forcing, the strain, the aspect of a weary man
seeking to fool us by strutting about in the regalia of
Chanticler — these "The Apple Cart" dins almost
continuously into our disappointed consciousness. For
Shaw remains a pet of so many of us, despite his
lapses, that we hope against hope, pull our thumbs for
him and are sorely dejected when he does not come
up to our loving demands of him. In these later days
there have been, alas, ample reason and occasion for
that dejection. For what are we old admirers to say
when, in this "Apple Cart," the first faint titter he can
work out of his audiences comes exactly *fifty minutes*
after the curtain on the first act has been raised and
when that titter is evoked by humor no fresher or no
more biting and profound than the observation that
when two persons are astride a horse one must sit behind the other, together with the thrice repeated query,
"Which?"

Throughout the evening, as hinted, this feebleness
persists, not only in the department of humor but in
the various other departments of dramatic writing.
The comic device of Boanerges' edging his way after
a pretty girl, only to have the door slammed in his face,
is one of the oldest standbys of the burlesque stage.
The singing of "For He's a Jolly Good Fellow," in the
situation that Shaw employs it, was one of the late

Raymond Hitchcock's favorite pieces of business for years. The understanding wife who soothes her troubled husband, pets him like a child and makes him eat his dinner quietly has already been worked to death by Hermann Bahr; it was the tag of a dozen or more plays before Shaw laid hold of it for this one. The mimicking of one character by another with a view to comic effect goes back to the dark ages and the episode wherein a man shows up at an important conference with a woman on each arm has been beloved of Palais Royal farce-writers for decades. (In Paris, it is usually a member of the Chamber of Deputies or the President of something or other; in "The Apple Cart" it is the King.) The servant who suddenly enters a boudoir and, seeing what he sees, puts his hands over his eyes and glides discreetly out of the door is hardly longer the material for considerable laughter. The timorous lover who, with his mistress' arms about him, gabbles about his wife, is a time-honored stencil of the farce stage. And so it goes, with a character named Lysistrata facetiously called Liz, an American, given the name Mr. Vanhattan, who shakes hands pump-handle fashion, the familiar injunction of one character to another to sit down, the silly female who giggles rapturously when a man tells her how attractive she is to the male sex, the character who works for comedy by dropping his hat, the joke about the modish look of a man who is dressed absurdly, and the joke about having to hurry back to the wife and children.

To sum up: The moments Shaw devotes to a paradoxical defense of constitutional monarchy — paradoxical merely because it is Shaw speaking — are
amusing. But the long hours he devotes to the em-
broidery of those moments are the hours of a genius'
clock that seems now at last to have stopped running.
Shaw is dead; long live the proud record of his youth,
a youth that deserted him only on his sixty-fifth birth-
day!

§ 9

*Ditto and Sex.*— Observes H. G. Wells in "The Way
the World is Going": "He (George Bernard Shaw)
has made free use of the phrase, the Life Force, but
what meaning he attaches to these magic words is un-
known. . . . He has an aversion from sex . . . which
may be either Butler or temperamental, and he seems
to want mankind to try laying parthenogenetic eggs,
and coming out of them fully whiskered."

The notion thus somewhat facetiously expressed by
the acute Wells restimulates a similar notion that for
some time has been impertinently agitating my en-
cephalon. That Shaw, as Wells says, appears not only
to have an aversion to sex but also what amounts almost
to a fear of it has not been lost upon those who have
carefully pondered his writings. The reason for the
peculiar aversion and for what seems to be even fear

is difficult to make out, but the antipathy and distrust nevertheless remain clearly visible and often emphatic. Shaw's canon plainly betrays his dislike of sex and his evasion of it. In all his work from beginning to end I know of no instance where he has not deftly avoided self-commitment on the subject or has not indulged in equivoque of one sort or another in his treatment of it.

It is impossible, within the limits of the present chapter, to go fully into Shaw's writings and draw from them a comprehensive catalogue of illustrations. But one may suggest the color of his intrinsic and general attitude by skimming through them and extracting a few sufficiently pointed and revelatory examples. That, when he laid hold of the incalescent Cleopatra, he chose to contemplate her at the age of sixteen and, in spite of the fact that sixteen was maturity in that gala era, insisted upon comfortably regarding her as a species of pre-Mary Pickford flapper, that he presented the Caesar who had a baby by her as an historical Crocker Harrington, and that he once achieved the remarkable feat of writing sexlessly about the madam of a bordello, are phenomena familiar to everyone. That, also, in the series of interviews gathered by Archibald Henderson into "Table Talk of G. B. S.," he orally betrayed an indifference, even antipathy, to sex is as readily recalled. I quote a few passages: (*a*) "It is admitted that alleged rejuvenations (*vide* Steinach) do not prolong life. And it is longevity which interests me and not the ghastly prospect of seeing all the moribund people bustling about and pretending to be gay young dogs"; (*b*) "There is never any real sex in romance. What is more, there is very little, and that of a very crude kind, in ninety-nine hundredths of our married life"; (*c*) "One man's poetry is another man's pruriency"; (*d*) "The novel which says no more about sex than may be said in a lecture on the facts to a class of school-girls of fifteen can be enormously more entertaining than a novel wholly preoccupied with sexual symptoms"; (*e*) "I could not write the words Mr. Joyce uses: my prudish hand would refuse to form the letters"; and (*f*) "Is any treatment of sex in the interest of public morals?" And where the interviewer shot embarrassingly direct questions on sex to the interviewed, the latter is remembered as having cleverly avoided direct answers in such circumlocutions as "A playwright has no patience with novels," or in disquisitions on economics, capitalism and what not.

Let us glance haphazardly through Shaw's work. Having presented us with a virginal Cleopatra and a Caesar whose amatory exercises are confined to lifting her upon his knee and playing horsie, he presents us with the inflammable Great Catherine as one of the Four Marx Brothers, and not Harpo either. He gives us a Pygmalion who will have none of his perfected Galatea and who, to use Shaw's own words, excuses his indifference to young women on the ground that they have an irresistible rival in his mother. "If an imaginative boy has a . . . mother who has intelligence, personal grace, dignity of character without harshness, and a cultivated sense of the best art, . . . she sets a standard for him against which very few women can struggle, besides effecting for him a disengagement of his affections, his sense of beauty and his idealism from his specifically sexual impulses. This makes him a standing puzzle to the huge number of uncultivated people . . . to whom literature, painting, sculpture, music and affectionate personal relations come as modes of sex if they come at all." He gives us even a Don Juan who moralistically announces, "I tell you that as long as I can conceive something better than myself, I cannot be easy unless I am striving to bring it into existence or clearing the way for it. That is the law of my life!" His Larry, in "John Bull's Other Island," prefers his friend Tom to the woman who implores his love. "I wish I could find a country to live in where the facts were not brutal and the dreams not unreal," is the character's oblique anatomical lament. His Dick Dudgeon, in "The Devil's Disciple," pronounces the word *love*, "with true Puritan scorn." His Lady Britomart, in "Major Barbara," "really cannot bear an immoral man." And his Eugene, in "Candida," romanticizes his emotions out of sex.

"Moral passion is the only real passion," announces

Tanner, in "Man and Superman." "All the other passions were in me before; but they were idle and aim-
less — mere childish greediness and cruelties, curiosi-
ties and fancies, habits and superstitions, grotesque
and ridiculous to the mature intelligence. When they
suddenly began to shine like newly lit flames it was
by no light of their own, but by the radiance of the
dawning moral passion. That passion dignified them,
gave them conscience and meaning, found them a mob
of appetites and organized them into an army of purposes and principles." "Virtue," Shaw notes in "The
Revolutionist's Handbook," "consists not in abstain-
ing from vice but in not desiring it." Charteris, in "The
Philanderer," accused of philandering, states that he
is not guilty of any such low thing. "I hate it; it bores
me to distraction!" Praed observes to Crofts of Mrs.
Warren, apropos of a hint of sexual intimacy, "Your
delicacy will tell you that a handsome woman needs
some friends who are not — well, not on that footing
with her." And Mrs. Warren repentantly thus: "Do
you think I was brought up like you — able to pick
and choose my own way of life? Do you think I did
what I did because I liked it, or *thought it right,* or
*wouldn't rather have gone to college* and been a lady
if I'd had the chance?"

Speaking of the marriage contract in one of his prefaces, Shaw alludes to sex stimulation as "the most
violent, most insane, most delusive and most transient

of passions," expresses his disbelief that married
people as a rule really live together, and says that "a
man as intimate with his own wife as a magistrate
is with his clerk . . . is a man in ten thousand." In
response to the General's timid "But there are calls of
nature —," in "Getting Married," Shaw makes Lesbia
reply, "Don't be ridiculous." And when the General
is so much as allowed to venture on another occasion
the word *assignation,* the Shavian get-out is accomplished thus: "Oh yes: she began the correspondence
by making a very curious but very natural assignation.
She wants me to meet her in Heaven" — the while
Mrs. Bridgenorth comments on the "everyday vulgari-
ties of earthly love." "I sinned in intention," says Juno
in "Overruled." "I'm as guilty as if I had actually
sinned." Lina, in "Misalliance," takes out her surplus
energy on a flying trapeze and recommends the same
diet to her adoring Tarleton. And in "Arms and the
Man," we find the Shavian protagonist not too proud
for sexual dalliance, but too tired.

The point is not that Shaw's imaginative writing is
sexless — that is a fact too well known to call for
repetition; the point is that the body of his work as a
whole reveals a man to whom sex, in the sense that
the word is commonly used, is at once unpleasant, deplorable and disgusting. There are times, true enough,
when he seems to advance the opposite point of view,
but it will be found that, when he does so, he does so

CHRONICLES

only subsequently to refute and demolish it. Nor is his argument of the other point of view even momentarily persuasive; it hasn't the ring of sincerity; it is a dummy set up merely for tackling purposes. Among conspicuous modern English men of letters and English critics of life, he alone is indefatigable in waving the white banner of biological asceticism. One of the cleverest dialecticians of our time, he is sometimes successful in concealing his true attitude for a moment, in masking his ferocious personal convictions and in giving a bland performance in the rôle of a hell of a fellow, but it fools no one. Chesterton once observed that it is the weak man who always, when taking a walk, most vigorously thwacks the bushes along the roadside with his cane. A mistrust of his own philosophical attitude toward sex may similarly account for Shaw's disputatious thwacking of it.

After reading "Cashel Byron's Profession," Stevenson wrote to William Archer: "If Mr. Shaw is below five-and-twenty, let him go his path; if he is thirty, he had best be told that he is a romantic, and pursue romance with his eyes open. Perhaps he knows it." Shaw is still the romantic that he was when a boy. And his romanticism is no more clearly to be detected than in his animadversions on sex. He declines to see it for what it is; he cannot bring himself to regard it save in terms of sentiment, love, the Indian policy, Marxian socialism or the League of Nations. And all the fine irony and rich humor which he occasionally has visited upon the subject cannot conceal the romanticist hiding behind them and seeking to protect himself through them from the charge of romanticism. Shaw has always set up smoke-screens or avoidances of the issue to protect himself from himself. The hero of his early novel, "The Irrational Knot," in answer to the query as to what he is going to do about his wife's elopement with a former lover, says, "Eat my supper. I am as hungry as a bear." His charming Szczymplica, in "Love Among the Artists," is in her potentially most romantic moments restrained by the "soul commercial" that Shaw, with a cannily masked apprehensiveness, injects into her. Lydia Carew, whose "body is frail and brain morbidly active," is made to think coldly of the splendid Cashel Byron in terms of eugenical science. In "An Unsocial Socialist," Shaw smears his inborn convictions with grease-paint and tries to make us believe that he believes the seven deadly sins, as Prof. Henderson notes them, are respectability, conventional virtue, filial affection, modesty, sentiment, devotion to women, and romance.

We have Shaw speaking of the wickedness and abandonedness of Offenbach's music and of the morals of Händel's. We find him waxing impatient with "the female figure free from the defect known to photographers as under-exposure" that he encounters on the statues and fountains in Paris. He writes, "What Hofmannsthal and Strauss have done is to take Clytemnestra and Ægistheus and by identifying them with everything that is evil . . . with the murderous rage in which the lust for a lifetime of orgiastic pleasure turns on its slaves in the torture of its disappointment and the sleepless horror and misery of its neurasthenia, to so rouse in us an overwhelming flood of wrath against it . . . that Elektra's vengeance becomes holy to us . . ." "In our sexual natures," he states in the preface to "Androcles and the Lion," "we are torn by an irresistible attraction and an overwhelming repugnance and disgust." Again, "Marriage turns vagabonds into steady citizens; men and women will . . . practice virtues that unattached individuals are incapable of." In the preface to "Overruled," thus: "That jealousy is independent of sex is shown by its intensity in children." Again, "Adultery is the dullest of themes on the stage, and from Francesca and Paolo down to the latest guilty couple . . . the romantic adulterers have been bores." Yet again, "It is ridiculous to say . . . that art has nothing to do with morality."

"If a young woman, in a mood of strong reaction . . . were to tell Mr. Herbert Spencer that she was determined not to murder her own instincts and throw away her life in obedience to a mouthful of empty phrases," he once said, "I suspect he would recommend the 'Data of Ethics' to her as a trustworthy and conclusive guide to conduct. Under similar circumstances I should unhesitatingly say to the young woman: 'By all means do as you propose. Try how wicked you can be. . . . At worst, you will only find out the sort of person you really are. At best, you will find that your passions, if you really and honestly let them all loose impartially, will discipline you with a severity your conventional friends . . . could not stand for a day.' " In the preface to "Getting Married," we come upon this: "The assumption that the specific relation which marriage authorizes between the parties is the most intimate and personal of human relations . . . is violently untrue." In "The Apple Cart," we engage the anatomically paradoxical spectacle of a King's platonic mistress. And, by way of a climax, we have a Garden of Eden in "Back to Methuselah" in which, when Shaw's Eve learns the secret of sex, "an expression of overwhelming repugnance" crosses her features and she "buries her face in her hands"!

# BOOK IV: LAMENTATIONS

## § 1.

*Drama.*— What literature does at night.

## § 2

*Dirt.*— There is no such thing as a dirty theme. There are only dirty writers.

## § 3

*The Pursuit of Diversion.*— The United States of the moment is amusement-mad to the point of insanity. In no other country in the world are a people so frantically engaged in the pursuit of diversion. The increased earnings of the masses following the late war have brought about a greater share of leisure and a greater urge and opportunity for play than have ever been enjoyed by the masses whether in America or elsewhere and, like sailors on a spree, the mob has gone on a wild pleasure drunk. There are more theatres in the United States today than in all the rest of the world combined. Tens upon tens of thousands of movie houses wind their unbroken chain from coast to coast. Jazz bands and dance halls overflow the cities and wash up into the smaller towns. Radios infest houses East and West, North and South. Cheap automobiles are found in almost every other back-yard. Circuses, carnivals and fairs crowd the countryside. Race-tracks flourish in every part of the land. Pleasure parks grow steadily in number; where a few years ago there was one, there are now a dozen. There are more and more new and larger bathing beaches; more and more road-houses; more and more public restaurants; more and more hotels for the increasing numbers of travel fiends. The boats to Europe are filled almost the whole year round and new boats are being rapidly built abroad to take care of the American crowds. Palm Beach, Havana, Nassau and the Winter resorts, once practically deserted, are now so packed at the first sign of frost that the wide, open spaces of a sardine can are roomy in comparison. Wherever one used to see a Carter's Little Liver Pill or Castoria sign from a rail-way-car window, one now sees a golf links, and every other former vacant lot is now a tennis court. Profes-sional baseball attracts bigger crowds than ever before and college football game tickets, even to stadiums holding seventy or eighty thousand people, sell at a substantial premium. There are ten times as many

speakeasies, beer flats and gin-sneaks in the country
as there were saloons in the old days. Small fortunes
are made by peddlers of hot-dogs on the motor highways, and the number of private swimming pools has
grown to Hollywood proportions.

Detective novels and other cheap literature are
gobbled up by the ton, and the sale of phonograph
records mounts steadily. Dance marathons, talking
derbys, six-day bicycle races, flag-pole-sitting and tree-
sitting contests, championship rocking-chair contests,
fairy balls, Tom Thumb golf and other such imbecilities are put into motion to satisfy the mob's hunger
for amusement of one kind or another. Bunion derbies
line the roadsides with diversion-seeking dolts. Hundreds of thousands of balls given by social and fra-
ternal orders, to say nothing of picnics, outings, excursions, clam-bakes and corn-roasts, enliven the
American night and day. Small traveling phonographs
grind out their melodies on countless trains, and home
movies are almost as common as musical cocktail
shakers. Moonlight bathing, hay-rides, hiking expedi-
tions and flying planes add to the pleasure-pushing picture. Ping-pong has come back into tripled flavor, and
contract bridge and backgammon have swept the country. Gum-chewing contests, pie-eating races, flea circuses and like divertissements of the lowly are more
popular than ever, and where there used to be one
street parade there are presently a dozen. Band con-

certs are a feature in every public square or park of any town of more than 25,000 inhabitants. The statistics show that there are thirty times the number of small power craft in use than there were ten years ago. Excursion boats do a thriving business, and the pocket flask industry is now second only to the movie industry. Three times as many cheap magazines are being published today as were published three years ago. And the Summer resorts, when warm weather sets in, are packed to the roofs.

With the enormous increase in the number and character of the public's amusements, the theatre has naturally lost a share of its former patronage. It is always a characteristic of entertainment madness to distribute itself widely rather than to centre itself upon a single relaxation, or even two or three forms of relaxation. The variety of games and diversions provided the inmates of an insane asylum is always much greater than that indulged in by the same number of normal men and women.

§ 4

*The Little Theatres and Sex.*— About the first thing that the average little, or art, theatre does — after it has sent out a Japanese vellum circular proving, to the presumable awe of the town's citizens, that its board contains a prominent local banker and society matron, neither of whom knows anything about drama — is to cast about for some new play, however bad, that treats of one of the more esoteric phases of sex. Unable for the moment to find such a play, it compromises for the time being with something by Strindberg in which a male and female use each other as punching-bags, with one of Wedekind's studies in abnormality or, by way of not letting the cat out of the bag too soon and antagonizing the banker and the society lady too greatly at the outset, with something somewhat more sexually *délicat* and *penseroso* by Schnitzler. These, however, are merely stop-gaps until some young man from the American cow-country or Paris Left Bank comes into the mails with a snappy little thing — calculated to jounce all true art lovers, and in particular those with dandruff — which deals with Lesbianism, algolagnia, masochism, voyeurism, illegitimacy, autoerotism, exhibitionism, rape, homosexuality, flagellation or incest.

It is an uncommon little art theatre, either up or down an alley, that does not seek at one time or another to yell itself into conspicuity with something that has no other reason for being save its sex cast. The argument advanced in behalf of its own glory by the little theatre in such cases is that the play in point is one that the professional theatre managers would be afraid of, although it is a matter of record that these professional managers have, with but a single exception, produced every actually meritorious sex play known to modern or classical drama — the exception, Wedekind's "The Awakening of Spring," having been given a hearing not by any little art theatre but by a group of professional actors. But, argument or no argument, the fact remains that the professional manager is never half so afraid of any radical sex theme as the little theatre playwright proves himself to be. The reason for this is pretty difficult to make out, but the truth remains. I know of hardly an exception to the rule. Tackling what seems to him to be a theatrically revolutionary sex theme, the little theatre playwright uniformly loses his nerve before he is half-way through with it and, by timid circumlocution and nervous reticence, causes it metaphorically to resemble the old-time adapted French farce in which what happened in the original was interrupted and forestalled by a ringing of the telephone, a knock on the door, or Herbert Corthell and Max Figman popping out from under the bed.

§ 5

*The Alley Drama.*— The thing that strikes the student of the alley drama most forcibly is not so much its strain to depart from the tradition and etiquette of the established drama as its strain to accompany that departure with a wealth of hoots, cat-calls, nosethumbings, smutty cracks and goddams. The average little theatre seems to believe that its mere juxtaposition to a cow-stable or Chinese laundry does something for it that could never be hoped for by a theatre anywhere near the Hotel Astor and it takes advantage of the fact — invigorated by the fresh breezes from the cow-stable and Chinese laundry — to snap the Muses' garters with a self-confident intimacy. The circumstance that Eugene O'Neill happened to get his start in one of these antipodean playhouses has encouraged a precocious corps of young men without any share of O'Neill's talent, save profanity, to let themselves go on the alley stages and to confound a gift for Billingsgate and a taste for anatomical radicalism with dramatic art.

Many of these closet theatres produce exhibits that are infinitely less plays than jeers at plays. Written by young men who haven't the slightest knowledge of dramaturgy, the stage shows abandon that art — much after the contemptuous manner of a pauper deprecating the cooking at the Ritz — and seek to conceal the Hobson's choice thus imposed upon them in a wealth of demented scenery, smoking-car studies in biology, allusions to women as sluts, views of dirty kitchen sinks, and stinging epigrams at the expense of Capital, legitimate babies and God, the whole retailed by the kind of actors who believe that there is something altruistically noble in playing tripe for twenty dollars a

week. It is only on rare occasions that these outhouses
of art display anything worth consideration. They began well enough and some years ago argued rather
eloquently for their place in the sun. They started out,
some of them, with excellent motives and not infrequently with commendable accomplishments. But in
the last few years they have made themselves ridiculous with the impudence that is ever the protective
coloration of impotence, and with exhibitions that are
little more than forensic turkey shows.

The outstanding defect of the little theatre movement generally in America is its self-imitativeness.
When the movement first got under way, there was
evident a fine impulse toward individuality, adventur-
ous enterprise and dramatic originality, and this impulse is still discernible in a few isolated little theatres
today. But what we see for the most part is simply
repetition, parroting: the little theatres have apparently resolved themselves into a chain of houses re-
producing much the same plays, much the same scenic
ideas and much the same tricks of lighting. One pat-
terns itself closely after the other; there is a minimum
of individuality and a maximum of copying. Once
fresh soil whence originated some of the fine things
in present-day American drama, scenic equipment and
lighting, there is now in the aggregate simply a somewhat snobbish and superficially cultivated little back-
yard garden, full of papier-mâché blooms.

## § 6

*Vox Brieux.*— It becomes increasingly evident that
many Anglo-American playwrights and producers outside the little theatres confuse equally a mere loud
statement of some hitherto theatrically unspoken phase
of sex with meritorious drama. In the last few years
we have had any number of inferior plays that would
surely never have got a hearing save for a scene in
their second acts wherein the heroine, elaborating upon
Houghton's Fanny Hawthorne, delivered herself of
some kind of sexual Trotzkyism or wherein the hero,
elaborating upon Brieux's physician, delivered himself
of some choice bits out of Marie Stopes. The theatres
have been filled with plays, none of them worth the
powder to blow them up, that have offered utterly
nothing in the way of drama but speeches proclaiming
the desirability of countenancing adultery to avoid
divorce, the justifiability of having babies out of wed-
lock, the merits of indiscriminate fornication, and the
idiocy of such rococo persons as still believe in the
common precepts of morality and decency. Once in a
blue moon a playwright comes along and, despite the
circumstance that he has a relatively new observation
to make on sexual conduct, yet remains mindful of the
fact that it is necessary for him to exercise some literary and dramatic skill in its development and pres-

entation. But, in the general run of things, our
playwrights seem to imagine that they can startle an
audience out of the consciousness of their immaturity
as craftsmen merely by booming suddenly into its ears
some hypothetically shocking anatomical philosophy.
The Anglo-American sex drama, on the whole, resembles nothing so much as a guinea-pig that has gone
intellectual.

§ 7

*The New Morality.*— While much that is true —
as it is equally obvious — has been written of the
so-called new morality in the English-speaking countries, an even more liberal share of buncombe has
found its way onto the stage and into print. For all the
contentions as to the comprehensive scope of the new
sex freedom, the unprejudiced observer notes that
the general attitude toward the situation in point is
largely the same as it was fifty and one hundred years
ago. While boys and girls and men and women may
each proclaim loudly that the old shackles no longer
bind them, it is still nasally unsafe to mention by name
any such girl or woman, whatever her self-expressed
and admitted independence, in the presence of any
friendly boy or man, for all his own self-expressed
and admitted emancipation in turn. Adultery is still
locally the one easiest and surest ground for divorce;

the unwritten law still wins the sentiment of ninety-
nine juries out of a hundred; the newspapers are richer
than ever in suits for what is euphemistically called
alienation of affections; an even hypothetically promis-
cuous woman is still socially *déclassée;* hotels still
insist upon at least one suit-case and duly eject any
couple that may come under the suspicion of moral
house-detectives; girls who do not return to their
dormitories by midnight or who are thought to have
been too friendly with the boys are still kicked out of
college; and a single illegitimate baby is enough to
make the editors of the tabloids, in convention as-
sembled, throw their hats into the air.

§ 8

*American-Made Comedy.*— American-made com-
edy, for all its occasional gift of entertainment, misses
the complete ease, or possibly the deftly concealed
uncertainty, of its British counterpart. There is a
periodic sense of strain to achieve an air of casualness
and there is evident also at times an unmistakable and
overpowering fear of the obvious. This latter persuades
the playwright to devices which, however handy, lose
much of their effect because of the transparency of the
labor involved in their manoeuvering. The playwright
gives one the impression of a street hawker who adver-
tises that he is going to show one a great novelty and

who, after a ballyhooing and rather clever bit of sleight-of-hand, opens his kit and displays for sale a mere stove polish. Thus, when one character is due to make a more or less stereotyped remark, the author seeks to take the edge off it by causing another ironically to anticipate it with "So you are going to tell me in all seriousness that two plus two equals four." This method of anticipation is common to American comedy. There is another purpose in it, also. It is employed by our writers to lend to their plays a superficial aspect of speed. It is a dodge, all too patent, to economize in the way of dialogue. Thus, "Don't say a word! I know what you are going to say. You are divorcing Cholmondely Plantagenet," is made to save not merely a line but often a long speech or two. Yet so open-and-shut and familiar is the trick that, instead of getting the effect desired, it misses completely because of its plain deliberation.

Casualness is one of the most difficult achievements in polite comedy. It is, of course, a matter of writing rather than a matter of acting or direction. Our playwrights sometimes manage it for part of the distance, but every now and again are so forcedly casual that one is made to think of the music show zany's nonchalance upon being told by his hostess that he had dropped some mayonnaise on his clothes. "Never matter," he returns with a quiet elegance, "I look well in anything I eat." There is a certain point up to which

the present diminished interest in the theatre doubtless lies in the circumstance that the drama of today is largely without what may be called heroine appeal. The heroine, in the old sense of the word, has practically disappeared from the drama, her place taken by an assortment of women lacking in anything approaching glamour and completely unalluring to the great majority of the public. If music show producers were to put on shows made up of deformed and ugly women, they would not be surprised to find that the public stayed away from them. But the legitimate producers seem to be shocked to find the public deserting their theatres when they, in turn, present an endless succession of plays with similarly unappealing pictures of womanhood.

The larger portion of the public goes to the theatre in quest of what, according to its lights, it regards as beauty, romance, spiritual fillip and glamour and these it seeks, after the tradition of centuries, in the embodiments of girlhood and womanhood that the drama may provide. Such consoling and satisfying embodiments it used to get, but no more. In the place of the noble and lovely heroines of yesterday it now finds an uninterrupted series of gutter prostitutes, flip flappers, Freudian mouthpieces, pseudo-Shavian chatterboxes and he-women, brash, brazen, wholly without charm and infinitely drab. And it is the same, to a but slightly lesser degree, with the heroes. What the drama cries

for is a return to spiritual swords and purple, to soft-
ness, fineness, gentle wonder and dignity. What the
drama needs are men and women of some romantic
warmth and beauty and not these common, swearing,
wisecracking, bawdy rats that today clutter up its
stage.

§ 10

*Supplementary Note to the Above.*— Back of the
statistics proving a great decrease in the marriage and
great increase in the divorce rates, both so learnedly
commented upon in a hundred and one quarters, there
is a small point, strikingly obvious, that has apparently escaped the attention of our friends, the philos-
ophers. That the relative disappearance of the romantic
impulse, due to the changing viewpoints as to sex and
morality, is in part responsible for the disruption of
the old order of things, is duly and truthfully recorded.
But one of the chief reasons for the disappearance of
that impulse on the masculine side seems to remain
unnoted. While it is more or less plain that woman's
increased economic independence, together with the
theorizing over a new moral code, the vanishing of
much of the old so-called home life and the psychic
unrest brought about by altered worldly conditions,
may in combination have done their full share in
changing the attitude of the sexes toward each other, it
is the masculinization of women, perhaps more than

anything else, that stands out as the disturbing fly in the molasses.

It is this acquired mannishness of women that has gradually converted a long sentimental and chivalrous order of men into a realistically minded and ironic body of cacklers. The romance that they once sought and found in women — a tradition of the centuries — they find no longer, for women more and more have ceased to be the figures of man's illusion and more and more have become superficially indistinguishable from man himself in his less illusory moments. In sport, in business, in drinking, in politics, in sexual deportment, in conversation, in sophistication and even in dress, women have come closer and closer to men's level and, with the coming, the gilt allure of distance has disappeared. Women act like men, talk like men, think like men; they wear men's tweeds and men's shirts and ties; they cut their hair short like men and use men's razors; they drink men's drinks and tell men's dirty stories; they sit in men's smoking cars and smoke men's tobacco; they jostle men in the voting booths and they wallop flirtatious fellows on the streets; they crowd men's golf links and tennis courts; they make the "dates" with men that men once made with them; they wear men's eyeglasses and brush their hair with military brushes; they go around in men's low-heeled shoes and they use men's cuss words; they swarm in men's places of trade; they write smutty books and read smuttier ones; they congregate, on land and sea, in bars and smoking-rooms hitherto reserved for men; instead of the old hat-pin they now use their fists; they bathe and swim in masculine bathing suits; they flock to prize-fights and yell enthusiastically at the sight of blood; they begin to talk sex before men get a chance to open their mouths; they wear pajamas, suspenders and knickerbockers; they ride horses cross-saddle and drive racing-cars and sweat at basketball; they carry men's cigarette cases and men's lighters and spit out bits of tobacco like men; they drive fast powerboats and airplanes and play the stock market; they go out alone at night and stay out; they laugh at virginity as they would laugh at a low burlesque-show joke; they know the exact ingredients of ergo-apiol. . . . And once upon a time there was a princess. "It was the blue of her eyes, that had the brightness of the Spring sky when there is no cloud anywhere between Heaven and the heads of men," writes Cabell, "which caused the armies of Rorn and of Ecben to meet like thunder clouds."

§ 11.

*Modernistic Scenery.*— That the crazy stage investiture which swept into the theatre some years ago, principally by way of Germany and Russia, is on its last legs and ready for the discard becomes increasingly apparent. I allude, of course, to the so-called impressionistic and expressionistic scenery sponsored by the arbitrarily radical wing, not to the carefully studied, relevant and immensely vital settings designed by such highly imaginative and honest fellows as Craig. That is, to the type of scenery employed by vainglorious designers to make a show for themselves at the expense of the drama, the kind of stage settings that substituted violence of line and color for self-effacing dramatic backgrounds and that diverted the attention of an audience from the drama and its actors with all the irritation of a loud nose-blow at vespers.

The stage seems already to have reverted again to normal; only on very rare occasions, and then not successfully, is the Caligari paint and canvas nonsense longer observable. We are back again where we were twenty years ago, but in terms of greater taste, greater skill and greater beauty. And the reason for the return to Bach is clear. Where the attempt to devise a new scenic idea fell down was in its failure to take into consideration the actor — the actor, that is, not as an actor but as a human being. The human being that was the actor stood out against the impressionistic and expressionistic backgrounds like a sore thumb; the one no more fitted in with the other than would a bass-drum with "Bilder Aus Osten." What we saw was scenic investiture that, while it distorted reality, made no allowance for the fact that what had to move in front of it were painfully real persons. As a consequence, the backgrounds howled against the actors and the actors against the backgrounds. All the while that we were looking at impressionistic and expressionistic houses, streets, skies and trees our eyes were bothered with decidedly unimpressionistic and unexpressionistic mimes. It was all very well to have backgrounds of lopsided magenta houses, red and yellow lamp-posts, triangular moons and orange zig-zag streets when the curtain went up, but it was something else to observe a few moments later, disporting himself before them, an everyday human animal in an everyday sack suit.

## § 12

*The Talking Pictures.*— The peak of imbecility, already sufficiently crowded with metaphysical mountain-climbers, finds its population lately augmented by a number of persons who profess to believe that the talking movies will spell the doom of the theatre. These persons are discovered to be the same ones who, ten years ago, scaled the heights with the conviction that the silent movies would spell the doom of the theatre. Arriving within reaching distance of the prize edelweiss, our friends observe themselves to be in the company of many of the old folks from home: the people who believed that the phonograph would kill

★ Be generous + keep in mind thru the next 14 sub-chapters that Mr G J Nathan was a drama critic, a playhouse goer, and a man not

the opera, the people who believed that the radio and the automobile would kill the theatre, the people who believed that ticket speculators and union labor demands would kill the drama, the people who believed that the tremendous increase in cheap magazines would kill the magazine business, the people who believed that the great oversupply of cheaply published books would kill the publishing business, the people who believed that the pianola would kill piano recitals, the people who believed that the elaborate rotogravure sections would kill the illustrated periodicals, and the people who believed that the big movie house orchestras would put an end to symphony concerts.

The talking pictures will have exactly the same effect on the legitimate theatre that the silent pictures had — that and no more. Indeed, unless I am more than usually mistaken, they will soon be found to have considerably less, and for a reason that seems to me to be plain. The silent movies appealed to that very considerable portion of the public whose intelligence was not up to the strain imposed upon it by the theatre in general. Such movies not only allowed that public to divert itself cheaply and without any other effort save that involved in keeping its eyes open, but permitted its imagination, such as it was, to function upon an agreeably low and apparently satisfactory level. What was more, the silent pictures were so fashioned that, no matter at what period during their

*given to a great love toward any substitute for a "living" theatre.*

course the customer entered, they were — because of the invariable periodic shrewd restatement of their plot schemes — clearly intelligible to him. This made it unnecessary for the customer to be in his seat at a particular time; he could drop in whenever he elected to and lose nothing — a valuable consideration in view of the fact that the movie public is not, due to its economic and social nature, chronologically so foot-free as the theatre public. In order to understand a talking picture, it is necessary for the movie patron to be present from the beginning, that is, save in the case of the musical comedy talkies. Nor is it reasonable to suppose that, by way of getting rid of this necessity, the talkie people will revert to the periodic plot restatements and thematic repetitions of the silent movie. Not only does the character of the new medium make that difficult, but to do so would be to render the talkie unbearably dull for such customers as had been on hand since the start. Oral repetition is involved and tedious, whereas a short printed recapitulatory title or a brief bit of pictorial pantomime is surely much less so. The talking picture, further, imposes upon its auditor much the same sort of strain that the theatre does: visually, aurally and every other way. And the better the talking pictures are, the greater the degree of that strain will naturally be.

The talking pictures, even imagining them in a future state of perfection, will obviously at their very best be mere theatre plays at second hand, and they will bear the same realistic approximation to drama that the poster of the celebrated musical comedy actress, in the ancient smoking-car story about the concupiscent country lout, bore to the servant girl under it. Where the silent movies gave the masses something that they could not find in the theatre, the talkies — except for some arbitrarily inserted train-wreck or avalanche — can give them only a ghostly copy of what they can find in the theatre.

The eminent Mr. Chaplin, who seems to have no use for the talkies, expresses it as his opinion that the latter, by their unavoidable sacrifice of sex appeal and visual beauty, will alienate the devotees of the silent movies in large numbers. The opinion strikes me as sound. The great popular success of the silent movies was unquestionably due to the mob's cigarette-picture adulation of their good-looking mimes and often to the aphrodisiacal quality which the mob imagined into them. Now, since nothing is less lovely to look at than photographs of a man's or woman's throat and jaw muscles in action and nothing less aphrodisiacal than speech, it is not difficult to anticipate the disillusion of the old fan audiences. Such devices as tricky camera angles and the soft focus, whereby piefaces were made to take on the aspect of Venuses, may not be applied to the liberal effect in the talkies that they were in the talkless pictures, and surely the censors will not permit the articulation of actions that once were freely allowed to inflame the imagination of the proletariat. The suggestion and glamour that inhered in the silent pictures are removed from the talkies, and the theoretical mystery that attached to their personages is doomed. The imagination-provoking shadows are discovered by the hinds to be simply very ordinary human beings with very ordinary human voices and with disturbingly conspicuous Adam's apples and cases of alveolodental periostitis.

The yokel who once imagined that the Mlle. Clara Bow, were she to whisper to him "I love you," would sound like a melted mandolin, now hears his goddess speak like a gum-chewing shop-girl. The worshipper of the Mlle. Mary Pickford's seductive girlishness now beholds her, in the grim, hard light of the talkies, to be a middle-aged woman with the voice of a middle-aged woman. The farmhand who once dreamed of the Mlle. Garbo as an exotic and mysterious dose of cantharides will now see her simply as a sizeable Swede with over-developed laryngeal muscles assisting in the negotiation of pigeon-English. Valentino died in time. Think what would have happened to his flock of women admirers if the unsparing lighting of the talkies had betrayed his imminent baldness and the movietone his banana-stand voice.

The talkies, even at their best, fall between two stools. On the one hand, they are not the scenic and pantomimic shadow movies of the past and, on the other, they are not the flesh and blood of the theatre. They miss the peculiar hypnosis of the silent pictures and they lack the human pull of the stage. Such persons as believe that the talking pictures may satisfy the ages-long pull of the living theatre are invited to reflect upon the great crowds of movie enthusiasts that invariably flock to the personal appearances of the movie stars. Curiosity to see such canned performers in the flesh is even greater than the curiosity to see them on the screen. The day that traffic isn't blocked when a Douglas Fairbanks and a Gloria Swanson go by will see the triumph of the screen over the stage.

### *b.*

What the phonograph is to opera, the lithograph to painting, the plaster of paris cast to sculpture and a doll's house to architecture, the talkie will ever continue to be to drama.

### *c.*

They say that in time they will so perfect the talkies that the present rasp and whirr will entirely disappear and the human voice will issue smoothly and naturally from them. They said the same thing about the phonograph many years ago and, for all the great improvement in it, the rasp and whirr are still there.

### d.

When there is a momentary end to conversation on the dramatic stage, the ensuing silence seems natural. But when there is a momentary end to speech in the talkies, the ensuing silence is grotesque and disturbing. The characters, once they have spoken, relapse simultaneously into muteness and screen dummies. They cease to be relatively real and become shadows again. The talking screen character and his other self, the silent screen character, are two different figures, and it is difficult for an audience to meld one with the other, to imagine both completely as the same being. Even a cursory view of the talkies impresses this fact upon the spectator.

### e.

One of the most difficult things on the stage, any actor will tell you, is reading and playing a scene effectively behind a scrim curtain. Even so thin and veil-like a substance interposed between the actor and the audience seems to take from the audience a sense of the actor's physical being and render him less a convincing, articulate creature of flesh and blood than a perplexing anomaly. If a mere strip of gauze can thus delete an actor's words and performance of persuasiveness and reality, what are we to expect of an actor's words and performance filtered through a thick film and a Westinghouse super-phonograph record?

*f.*

The reason for the dissatisfaction of a considerable share of the old silent movie customers with the talkies doubtless lies in the fact that the talkies are at their best a mere cuckooing of theatrical drama. The silent movies were more often a thing apart from theatrical drama, and hence offered the customers a different form of entertainment. Those customers could go to the theatre if they desired to, or to a movie if they desired to, and each gave them something distinctive, however bad. Today, with the silent movies gone, the customers have, to their way of thinking, only one form of diversion left to them: the spoken play. The novelty of the talkies' mechanism has already begun to wear off for them, and only the mock theatre play remains. Where once they had two essentially different ways to spend two evenings, they now have but one.

*g.*

The last word in movie nonsense is what is designated by the entrepreneurs as "cinematic descriptive music," demonstrations of which have recently been vouchsafed the art-lovers who frequent the various film palazzos. This cinematic descriptive music is, as the phrase implies, a combination of descriptive music and moving picture, the latter illustrating with hypothetically appropriate pictorial monkeyshines the progress of the composition. Thus, Saint-Saëns' "The Swan," which purports to suggest the movements of a swan in terms of melody, is keyed to an accompanying movie which shows a swan or two in action, the swan or two in point being unfortunately somewhat deficient in musical understanding and conducting themselves in a manner most disturbing to the M. Saint-Saëns' idea of what is swanly seemly.

So-called descriptive music, as Polichinelle has long been aware, is generally more or less integrally asinine and has needed only this new adjunct to constitute it perfect moron entertainment. Within the year we shall doubtless see Rubinstein's "Barcarolle" accompanied by a movie of Central Park rowboats, Liszt's "Gondoliera" helped out by a Pathé travel film of Venice, Chopin's "Ballade in G Minor" pictured by a Hollywood actor dressed up as Konrad Wallenrod, and Beethoven's "Sonata in F Minor" illustrated by views of Vesuvius in eruption, together with a news reel showing panoramic pictures of the year's most disastrous railroad and automobile wrecks.

*h.*

The stupidity of the talkie director is no more

clearly to be observed than in his continued use of the close-up. The close-up was introduced into the old silent movie as an unavoidable necessity. Without the spoken word it had often to be relied upon to convey to an audience, through an intimate view of a character's play of features, that character's momentary mood and implied thought. With the addition of the spoken word to the screen, the device obviously no longer has any reason or sense, yet the directors, lacking in the faintest trace of imagination, have not thought to discard it.

*i.*

One of the damaging effects that the talking moving pictures will have on the dramatic theatre will be the histrionic corruption, at least temporarily, of the numerous competent legitimate actors and actresses who are resorting to them by way of making more money than the theatre can afford to lay out. This damaging effect, I have no doubt, will be clearly evident when these actors and actresses return to the stage from their Klondike holiday. Talkie acting, for its best effect, calls upon the most obvious and artificial tricks in the mummer's craft; subtlety in any degree is dangerous; the best actor or actress in a talkie is the one who, were he or she to act the same play on the stage in the same manner, would be the worst. The acting values of the stage, voice excepted, are turned hind-end foremost in the talkies. If the late Jeanne Eagels, whose performance in the talkie version of "The Letter" was highly praised by the talkie experts, were to have played "The Letter" in the theatre in the manner she acted it on the screen, the audience would have let out a yell as loud as would be that of a talkie audience at the screened spectacle of Grace George's excellent performance in "The First Mrs. Fraser."

The legitimate player who sticks to the talkies for any length of time will naturally and inevitably reacquire all his early bad acting tricks or acquire a lot of bad ones that he has not had before. Look at any one of these players in even his first talkie and you will already thus soon see the dismal streaks putting in an appearance. Exaggeration, face-making, overemphasis necessary to register effects in the back reaches of the spacious movie cathedrals, awkward pauses to time action and dialogue to the movie public's slow perceptions, an altered carriage to suit the constricted talkie stage — these will be brought back to the dramatic theatre when the truants return. And, as acquired evils are not quickly got rid of, the theatre is, accordingly, destined for some time after that return to witness acting beside which that of the late lamented John McCullough and the Cherry Sisters was full-blown genius.

### *j.*

It occurs to me that if the talking moving pictures have any sense they will concentrate not so much upon speech as upon those sound effects that are and always have been so immensely effective in the theatre and in drama. While speech must inevitably be a more or less anomalous thing on the screen, sound effects may fit it aptly and they must just as inevitably add to the pictures' relative impressiveness. Some of the most vivid and expedient moments in the dramatic theatre have been achieved not by the human voice but by sounds of another and quite different character — and even so far as the human vocal chords are concerned there is and has been little so dramatically startling and moving, time on end, as a mere inarticulate shriek.

Sounds unrelated to the human voice, that the moving pictures can handily incorporate, have long brought to drama a dynamic power that has added to its effectiveness. The clicking of the time-bomb in such a melodrama as "The Fatal Card" had in it a quality of mounting, nervous suspense that no human speech could induce in an audience. The tom-tom poundings in "The Emperor Jones," the bells in "The Bells," the fog-horn in "Bound East for Cardiff," the swish of the sea in "The Moon of the Caribbees," the slowly approaching and doomful tread of feet in "The Gods of the Mountain," the rumble of the train in "Clarice," the clicking of the telegraph instrument in "Secret Service," the crescendo of boat sirens and whistles swelling in counterpoint to the gradually bursting emotions of the characters in "Strange Interlude," the ominous Oriental piping and the clanging of the iron shutter in "The Speckled Band," together with the clanking of the door chains of Moriarty's cellar in "Sherlock Holmes" — where will you find more legitimate attributes and promotions of dramatic effect? Let the movies abandon the hope of contending with the drama with speech, keep their pantomimists silent and go after a share of the theatre's kick with the stage's exciting noises. There is often more elemental thrill in the sound of approaching horses (cocoanut shells or no cocoanut shells), more ecstasy in the sound of a piano in an upper room (as in Fulda's "Jugendfreunde"), and more valid elemental drama in the sound of a gradually growing-faint locomotive whistle (as in "Forty-five Minutes from Broadway") than in the larynxes of half the actors in Christendom.

*k.*

Sound is a legitimate adjunct of the moving picture and has been since the first. The present machines have simply taken over, elaborated upon and made more realistic the old orchestra drum wallop to signify a train crash, the old rap on the triangle to signify a striking clock and the old scraping on a 'cello string to mimic a cow's mooing. But the spoken word is no more honestly a part of the moving picture than it is part of the mimetic art of the ballet.

### *l.*

Until they so perfect the talking picture machine that they can take the close-up of a word — a word in all its subtle shadings, whispered graces and meaningful inflections — drama in any save the most elemental sense must remain a stranger to the screen.

### *m.*

It is refreshing to observe that, thus far, none of the movie magnificoes has come forth with any high-sounding art gabble about the talkies. In the relatively brief reign of the silent pictures we were familiar with a wealth of such nonsense as "The moving picture is the art form of the future"; "The motion picture is an art that will endure long after all the other arts are dead," etc., etc. Having apparently learned their lesson, the movie people have gathered around the cold corpse of their previous "art" and are now simply grabbing their pay envelopes from the talkies, keeping mum, and leaving talk about art to artists.

## n.

A half dozen years ago, I wrote that the moving pictures*would not last, that it was ridiculous to use the word art in connection with them, and that they would sooner or later pass into limbo. The statement was jeered and I was set down a fool.+Where is the old moving picture today? It is as dead as a doornail; it has disappeared from the scene almost completely. Emboldened, therefore, I make another prediction that will doubtless meet with the same jeers and with the same derogation of my clairvoyant gifts. It is this: that the talkies will sooner or later go the way of the silent movies. The talkies, even at their best — though what that is, I haven't from personal experience of them discovered — are merely second-hand theatre drama and musical comedy. They will not long satisfy audiences, for all their relatively cheap admission prices, for audiences, low or high, have a way of disliking any substitutes for any real thing. The road was partly killed by second companies in place of the original companies. And the best talkie is inevitably, by its intrinsic nature, a road version of theatre drama. The old movie audiences, at the height of the silent movies' success, never failed to go out of their way for so much as a glimpse of one of the movie actors or actresses. The present talkie audiences have got a step nearer to intimacy with their favorites through the

*silent pictures*

*+ Mr. Nathan is not being honest. The "talkies" killed the "silents", and nothing else.*

*≠ The Same GJN that said all this would today (1952) be predicting Tv won't last.*

added medium of speech, but they still want to see
them in the flesh. And one of these days they will all
have to go back to the theatre to see them thus.

§ 13

*The Provincial Bier.*— To believe that it is bad
plays that have killed what is known in theatrical
parlance as the road — the contention of the majority
of critics — is to have a magnificent faith in the sudden achievement of aesthetic perception on the part
of millions of Americans. It might be well to call the
attention of these critics to the fact that the road was
in its heyday when the fare it got consisted of such junk
as "The Old Homestead," "Ben Hur," "Way Down
East," "The County Fair," "A Parlor Match," "Ten
Nights in a Bar-room," "The Shepherd King," "A
Trip to Chinatown," "The Gladiator," "Christopher,
Jr.," "The Eagle's Nest," "The Charity Ball," "Dark-
est Russia," one-bloodhound "Uncle Tom" troupes,
"Trilby," "Blue Jeans," "The Heart of Maryland,"
"Shenandoah," "Because She Loved Him So," "The
Lost Paradise," "The Coronet of the Duchess," "A
Fool of Fortune," "David Harum," "The White
Slave," "The Helmet of Navarre," "Virginius," "In
Old Kentucky," "The Count of Monte Cristo," "Mlle.
Mliss," "Are You a Mason?", "All on Account of
Eliza," "Quo Vadis," "Mice and Men," "On and Off,"

and "A Poor Relation." When the road was at the height of its glory, the plays were at their very worst. For every meritorious new play or revival of a classic that the average American road city got, it got a dozen beside which such low dishes and failures of this last season as "Suspense," "Insult" and "Roadside" were authentic works of art. The theory, furthermore, that large numbers of erstwhile theatregoers in the hinterland have deserted the theatre for the talking pictures must be believed chiefly by such persons as are persuaded that men and women whose taste is for the drama, however seldom that taste may be gratified with something worthwhile, can possibly be interested in the talking pictures even as a periodic diet. If such men and women don't go to the theatre, they stay at home. Certainly no film house gets them.

## § 14

*Plot.*— A re-reading today of Conan Doyle's celebrated Sherlock Holmes series brings one to a puzzled pondering of the enormous success that the stories enjoyed in their time. Read again after many years they not only seem very bald and crude in a literary direction, but for the most part ingenuous in their plot schemes. Holmes himself, though grantedly the most popular and most widely known character in modern fiction, is seen to be a character less of Doyle's creation than of Doyle's readers. Holmes, so far as Doyle's character analysis goes, is the merest shadow. His double-peaked cap, hypodermic needle and pipe apparently mark the limits of the author's power of character delineation. His speech is without definite mark or illuminating idiosyncrasy; his musings are associated solely with the hide-and-seek plots in which he is made to figure and disclose next to nothing of the man himself; his actions are the arbitrary actions of tin-pot melodrama. And so far as his outward aspect goes, it is suggested to the reader not by Doyle but by the illustrator, Steele, who drew the pictures for the stories. It is, in point of fact, Steele's Holmes rather than Doyle's that people visualize when they think of the detective.

The only explanation that one can advance for the great success of the Holmes stories lies not in their writing, which is bad, nor in their character delineation, which is worse, but in their plot appeal. For all the insistence of professorial literary criticism that it is character rather than plot that makes for longevity in the field of fiction, we have here still another example in contradiction. Action that makes character, however indeterminate the character may be, has a greater and wider popular appeal than the finer literature in which character determines action. Robinson Crusoe, Uncle Tom, Little Red Riding Hood and dozens of other such plot-born characters continue, like

Sherlock Holmes, to enrapture and engross the public, where characters who are parents of their plots do so in minor degree. Holmes was and is a world success not because of himself but simply because he happened to be present when a shudderful hound howled on the dark moor, when a poisonous and terrifying snake crawled down a bell-cord, and when a deadly Hindu dart was projected from a blow-pipe.

## § 15

*Mystery.*— That there is at the moment an almost world-wide palate for plays, talking pictures and fiction of the so-called mystery species is plainly apparent. The reason for the phenomenon isn't any too easy to get at. While it may be true that there is always a measure of popular interest in mystery and detective pastime, never before has the interest been so uniformly widespread and so great. Like any attempt to explain such things, the business of figuring out a reason resolves itself largely into a guessing contest. Of such guesses I have, after a herculean ponderation that has shaken me to the very bowels, given birth to no less than a dozen, each successively impressing me as worse than the other. By way of establishing my ineptitude at parlor games, I append a few typical deductions:

Result of analytical meditation No. 1: Of all forms

of entertainment, the mystery play or story most greatly flatters the cerebral vanity of persons without minds, in that it challenges the superficial brain cells with a showy substitute for ratiocination.

Result of analytical meditation No. 2: The late war produced killing on such an enormous scale that, by virtue of its very magnitude, that killing became in turn incomprehensible and neuter, much as a surplusage of alcoholic drink becomes tasteless or as grief over a long period has a way of becoming mechanical and emotionally static. Killing on the grand scale became an impersonal thing and such is human nature that it lost personal interest. And, as the murder of a single citizen is always closer to the interest of the people in a town than the killing of thousands of men on some far battlefield, the public's emotions craved a reduction of murder, a narrowing down of murder to a point of personal interest and personal sympathy. There have not been enough spectacular murder stories in actual life to satisfy the public — since the war there have been only two in England, one in France, one in Germany and seven in more enterprising America — and the murder plays, talkies and novels have been gobbled up by way of vicarious satisfaction. The public, not seeing or knowing personally the tens of thousands of men killed in battle, could not feel half the personal concern in their murder that it can feel in the murder of an actor it lays eyes on or even in the murder of a character that a novelist has made intimately real to it.

Result of meditation No. 3: The mystery play has much the same quality as a baseball game, a horse race or any other such popular competitive sport. Its excitement for the spectator lies in betting upon and determining the name of the ultimate winner. Everything is intensely directed toward the finish, the solution, the award. Most other forms of drama lack this measure of nervous suspense, as they rely more upon the casual playing of the thematic game itself than upon the conclusion. The play other than the mystery play is not so greatly concerned with its outcome as with its intermediate by-play. It appeals to the relative minority who go to a horse race more because they love horses than because they admire jockeyship.

Result of meditation No. 4: The mystery play, the world over, presently occupies the fancy of the generation of audiences that has grown up since the outbreak of the late war and that, while it has outgrown childhood, is still not yet completely adult. Before the war these audiences, then at the sapling age, found delight in an endless success of stage magicians, illusionists, prestidigitators and quick-change artists, such followers of Houdin and Hermann the Great as Maskelyne, Kellar, Fregoli, Carter, Thurston, Houdini, Conradi, the Baldwins, Mercedes, the Zanzigs, Anna Eva Fay, Ching Ling Foo and a host of others. The next theatrical rung after the magician, mind-reader and general goldfish-bowl hocus-pocus artist is the mystery play and the child-adult audiences, in the natural slow sequence of growth, are currently engrossed with it.

Result of meditation No. 5: The public relishes the mystery play because it substitutes out-and-out plot for more or less shadowy and involved theme. The theme play develops out of itself slowly: what it is driving at is made only gradually to sink into the consciousness of an audience. But the mystery play states its intrinsic nature plainly soon after the curtain goes up, thus relieving the audience of metaphysical speculation and permitting it lazily and comfortably to enjoy its mental shortcomings in cross-word puzzle details.

All of which probably does not account in any way for the present great success of mystery plays, books and talkies.

§ 16

*Art and the Clown.*— Writing of the comedian, Ed Wynn, a fellow-critic works himself up as follows: "He has never seemed so indisputably great as he does this time in the full ripeness of his art — not merely an expert musical stage comic, although it is essential that he should always be that, but an artist

who lifts his tomfoolery into the realms of fantasy."
While no one admires this Wynn's comic talents more
than I do, just where such things as "indisputably great
in the full ripeness of his art" and "an artist who lifts
his tomfoolery into the realms of fantasy" figure in
connection with riding a gilt bicycle, coming out in a
series of funny hats and showing the audience a patent
cigarette lighter with a box of matches attached to it,
I am evidently much too dumb to appreciate. Wynn is
certainly a good clown and he can certainly make me
laugh along with all the others in an audience, but if
the realms of fantasy have anything to do with him, or
he with them, Maeterlinck and Hofmannsthal wasted
time away from the Mack Sennett lot. This business of reading high art into low comedians does not
seem to let up. In the last seven or eight years, at least
a dozen zanies have been pounced upon by our critics
and have been made to keep embarrassed company
with Salvini, Botticelli and Brahms. Charlie Chaplin,
Joe Cook, Harpo Marx, Harold Lloyd, Frank Tinney,
Beatrice Lillie, the late Bert Williams and any number of other such entertainers have been greased,
anointed, hymned and drummed up to a point where
nothing was left over to be said for authentic genius.
Wynn is now getting his dose. I only hope that it will
not spoil him as it has certain other comiques. It would
be a shame to lose such a gay clown and get in his stead
simply another puffed-up and self-conscious actor.

## § 17

*Matinée Idols.*— The matinée idols of another generation who are still with us disclose themselves to be the same atrociously bad actors that they always were. Products of the pre-John Gilbert, pre-Gary Cooper era, they initially came into prominence through the servant-girl school of criticism that obtained at the time, not because they knew how to act but simply because they were six feet tall, had a lascivious eye-wink and were presumably gifted with It. The Alan Dales, Acton Davieses and other such interpreters of matinée *Kultur* in those years hailed them much as their facsimiles of today hail the movie facsimiles of them, not on grounds of histrionic competence but on grounds of theoretical amatory talent.

## § 18

*The Mime Past Sixty.*— After an actor passes sixty his ambition is generally to play either the rôle of a gay young Lothario or of a man so old that he can hardly get up from a chair without suffering a stroke of apoplexy. Such rôles flatter his vanity, the first obviously enough and the second because the great age of the character makes his own seem relatively tender. Thus we have had Irving in "Waterloo," Arliss in "Old English," Maude in "Grumpy" and a score of other such patriarchs attempting to conceal their personal senility from the consciousness of audiences through the subterfuge of a doubly senile make-up, and thus we recently had Mr. Otis Skinner up to the same trick in "A Hundred Years Old." More often than not, the death of the ancient at the end of the play is permitted to make even more emphatic by contrast the life that still lingers miraculously in the actor. Mr. Skinner, somewhat more modest, apparently, than other histrionic violets, did not allow himself to die, but in other respects he pleasured himself with all the familiar coggery of exaggerated dramatic senescence.

In the field of his art, this Mr. Skinner has never impressed me as being the highly capable mummer that certain of his admirers maintain him to be. He has given a couple of fair performances, in "Kismet" and in "The Honor of the Family," but his work in these plays as well as in everything he has ever done has been cut to a single, invariable pattern. His performance, whatever the nature of a rôle, is always exactly the same. If he is playing a bristling French colonel or a whining Arabian beggar, a vigorous harvester or a Spanish centenarian, he relies upon the same manner of speech, the same intonations, the same repeated proddings with a walking stick, the same physical comportment and the same face-makings to interpret the rôle. Take his vocal organs, for example, which he seems to regard much as a player in a Negro band regards a saxophone, that is, not as an instrument with which to play a composition but as something with which to indulge in a lot of extraneous monkeyshines. Mr. Skinner does not read a dramatist's lines; he merely makes noises with them. Now he moos like a pensive cow; now he issues tremolo sounds like a wistful chorus man; now he growls like a bear; periodically he smacks his lips and clicks his tongue, following which he debonairly trills little scales; occasionally he gargles and chokes; and then again he moos. I am not averse to such imbecilities, but Mr. Skinner, if he wishes to indulge in them, should pick his plays more appropriately — or have the Minsky Brothers pick them for him.

§ 19

*Chair Acting.*— One of the established sure-fire figures of drama and comedy is the character of the hobbling, querulous and ironically sharp-tongued old lady who sits in an armchair for the major portion of the evening and points her remarks with a cane. This personage, whether female or male, has long been a recognized figure in the stage character gallery and, for all its familiarity, never fails to draw praise from the critics for its excellence of portraiture, however commonplace its execution may be. And the actress or actor who plays the character, whether good or bad, invariably shares in that praise. From the day that Henry Irving presented himself as the doddering old man in a dramatization of Conan Doyle's "Story of Waterloo" — a performance truthfully characterized by Shaw as the veriest histrionic flapdoodle — critics have deluded themselves into accepting as examples of stunning virtuosity performances that impose no more strain upon an actor's talents than that involved in applying a pint of makeup to his face, making his voice quaver and periodically converting his knees into seismographs. "Enter Mr. Irving," wrote Shaw, "in a dirty white wig, toothless, blear-eyed, palsied, shaky at the knees, stooping at the shoulders, incredibly aged and very poor, but respectable. He makes his way to his chair and can only sit down, so stiff are his aged limbs, very slowly and creakily. This sitting down business is not acting; the call-boy could do it; but we are so thoroughly primed . . . that we go off in enthusiastic whispers, 'What superb acting! How wonderfully he does it!' . . . Every old actor will wish that he could get such press notices for a little hobbling and piping and a few bits of mechanical business. . . . The whole performance does not involve one gesture, one line, one thought outside the commonest routine of automatic stage illusion. What, I wonder, must Mr. Irving, who of course knows this better than anyone else, feel when he finds this pitiful little handful of hackneyed stage tricks received exactly as if it were a crowning instance of his most difficult and finest art? . . . But the critics!"

And what must Mr. Arliss feel, and Miss Granville, and all the score and more of other actors and actresses who, after laboring for years, find acclaim from the critics at last only when they similarly put on gray wigs, hobble around on canes, sit down in wheel-chairs, talk the way the Three Giersdorf Sisters sing and so persuade the critics that they are great character interpreters? Not only are such paint-and-powder char-acters the easiest to act but undoubtedly the easiest, as well, to write. It is the hack plays that have contained most of the best of these so-called characters, if we are to accept the critics' valuations of the latter. The audi-ence effect is automatically achieved the moment the old boy or girl is revealed in his or her chair. Sitting there and dryly commenting on the other actors who are made to leg it hither and thither like so many chip-munks, the character works on the audience much in the way that William Gillette shrewdly used to when he caused all the rest of the company to read their lines like college yells while he himself stood tranquilly to one side and read his in a soft and even voice.

## § 20

*Sex and the Actress.*— One of the only ways to in-terest anyone in obvious sex plays is, clearly enough,

to engage for the rôles of the sexualists women sufficiently aphrodisiacal to make the whole business seem
somewhat plausible. Otherwise no one gives a hoot
what happens to them or is in the least concerned with
their amatory excitements.

§ 21

*The English Actor.*— The old affection of American
theatrical audiences for English actors — an affection
that reached almost the height of amorous passion
during the Charles Frohman régime — seems to be
cooling off so rapidly that the day is probably not
distant when London performers will practically disappear from the local stage. Now and again, of course,
a single English actor of some talent may continue to
be received with favor, but that the English actor in the
mass is no longer *persona grata* over here is painfully
apparent. The way the wind is blowing was clearly to
be perceived in the instance of four of the more recent
importations of English companies and the receptions
accorded them. The British actors and actresses in
point, representative of the English player by and
large, were either openly mocked or politely disparaged. In the case of at least three of them, loud and open
laughter was the portion. And the reason is not difficult
to get at. There are, on the English stage, a fair number
of actors and actresses highly skilled in their art and

expert in speech and human in stage deportment. But
for every such one, there are a hundred who are carica-
tures not only of actors but of human beings and of
funnels of English speech. It is these, unfortunately,
who most often come to America and who increase the
American prejudice against the British stage profession
as a whole. It is these who with their accordion-pleated
trousers, bib-waistcoats and other such sartorial lam-
poons, with their affected gait and Bloomsbury version
of *savoir faire,* and with their *lahvelys* for *lovely,*
*deahs* for *dear, rawthers* for *rather, tahchs* for *touch,*
*pots* for *part, hyahs* for *here, payatrys* for *poetry,*
*pawssibles* for *possible, wares* for *were* and *welds* for
*world* make themselves, the plays they play in and
their profession ridiculous and who have brought their
clan into comical disrepute. They are not Englishmen,
but burlesques of Englishmen; they are not actors, but
burlesques of actors.

There was a time, as I have hinted, when the inex-
perience and cheap snobbery of American audiences
combined to work for an acceptance of such mountebanks as the real and rather tony thing. But that time
is past. The American theatrical audience of today, its
cheapest element drafted from it by the talkies, is a
more traveled audience, a more cynical audience and
a more sagacious one. And it has come to recognize
these absurd imposters and counterfeits for what they
are, to wit, woeful incompetents who seek to mask

their acting incompetence in external pseudo-fashionable monkeyshines, much as expert waiters in the more elegantly decorated restaurants mask the inferiority of what they serve by the elaborate hocus-pocus of their service. With that recognition, the doom of the English actor in the aggregate has been spelled and it will not be long before he may be expected to disappear from the American scene. For the English actor of position there will still be a place, but for these London dummies and bastardizers of the English language there will be only obscene mouth-noises.

It is not, obviously, that the American actor, unlike the English actor, always speaks the English language with a high and beautiful purity. He surely does nothing of the kind. But the difference is that he is generally seen in plays, unlike the English actor, that make no demand for clear enunciation and pronunciation, and hence gets away — not improperly — with what would otherwise be his striking deficiencies. He plays in underworld plays, crook plays, Flatbush and Bronx genre studies, slangy comedies and farces, college plays, speakeasy melodramas and plays of a loose-lipped kind and his shortcomings in the way of perfect English speech are not apparent. He is most often called upon to be the oh-yeah, sez-you, keep-your-nose-clean species of actor, whereas his English brother, by the same average, is of necessity of the politer species. Even in the English underworld and

crook plays the language demanded of the latter has
its modish shadings; certain of the underworld characters in Mr. Edgar Wallace's recent attempt at a Chicago
gunman drama, a great success in London, are peculiarly bidden by the author to conduct their speech much
after the manner of Frederick Lonsdale actors. In addition, the poor speech of American actors is largely
taken for granted by American audiences and condoned, much as family faults are ever condoned. But
the English actor's speech, once ignorantly believed to
be the acme of perfection, now that it has been found
out by American audiences to be merely bad Cockney
in swallowtails is not only not thus condoned but is
regarded as something — to quote Mr. Peter Arno —
not only unaesthetic but lousy.

I have seen a number of English actors on the London stage who know their jobs perfectly and who know
how to speak their language beautifully. But we do not
often see that kind over here. They stay at home and
what we get in their stead are a pack of acting pre-
tenders suitable only for the rôles of English butlers
in American farces.

The popularity of the American actor in England,
apparently a paradox, is perhaps to be explained in
several ways. The American actor who plays over
there is most often seen in American crook, slang and
wisecracking exhibits, to which his speech is perfectly
fitted and in which he seems, quite rightly, to English

audiences to be absolutely and perfectly at home. When he appears in London in plays of a different stripe, plays that call for a purer pronunciation and enunciation, his success is due simply to the fact that the more cultured Britons in the stalls, who have been surfeited with and sickened by so much Bloomsbury-ism passing itself off for Mayfair, are overwhelmingly delighted to get a whiff of something natural, something unaffected and something that even remotely approaches correct English speech. In no other way can we explain the success in London of a considerable number of American actors and actresses who were rank failures in their own land and who, many of them, had to go to London to get the jobs that no producer would think of giving them here.

§ 22

*Actors.*— Actors who seek to convey a granite personality by growling like a stomach full of sour apples . . . blond, marcelled, overly tailored and aggressively self-satisfied musical comedy leading men whose air of excessive swelldom is somewhat invalidated by their habit of rubbing their hands at such moments as they are called upon to express great elation and of pointing a finger roguishly at the object of their affection as the orchestra strikes up some such song as "It's You, Suzette, I Love" . . . other such

LAMENTATIONS                    231

actors who try to persuade an audience that they have
the volume of Chaliapin by stealthily puffing out their
bosom shirts before they go into a song number and
by opening their mouths on the last note to some imaginary giant of a dentist . . . actresses as ferociously ingénue as Henry Wadsworth Longfellow . . .
actresses who suggest nonchalance by a contumelious
puffing at a cigarette and nervous impatience by crossing their legs and restlessly agitating their right foot
in the manner of someone desperate for the ladies'
room . . . Actors with newspapers carefully hung
out of their side pockets to indicate homeyness and unaffected simplicity, with periodic lusty knee and thigh
slappings to suggest great geniality and with every
other line followed by a heavily manufactured but
theoretically lovable little chuckle . . . actresses who
have been told by someone that natural acting consists
in a sedulous avoidance of everything even faintly associated with the art of acting . . . actresses who de-
pict tough women by putting their hands on their hips
and undulating their rears . . . actors whose idea of
*sang froid* is to speak in a voice so refinedly pianis-
simo that no one can make out what they are saying . . . actors who portray impulsiveness by stepping forward suddenly with the right foot and then
vibrating the left leg . . . negresses in musical shows
who elaborately roll their eyes and clap their bottoms
under the impression that they are twice as sexually

electrifying as white girls who conduct themselves
somewhat more sedately. . . .

## § 23

*Home Grounds.*— With one or two recognizable
exceptions, the American playwright of today, whatever his share of talent, is to be commended for stick-
ing so uniformly to subjects and characters that he
knows best and most intimately. There was a time
when he sought to give an air to his wares by apeing
the English and the French, whether in the way of
themes or alien characters, with the result that he
made a monkey of himself as a man ever does when
he tries to do something that is not in his ken to do.
A writer with no knowledge of French, say, should
never so much as employ a single French phrase, however stereotyped, for he fools no one as to his linguistic
parts. He may use the phrase with complete accuracy,
yet there remains something — just what it is is hard
to define — that betrays a certain lack of ease and
makes him seem affected. So with a playwright. An
American may put the character of an English lord,
let us say, into his play and make a superficially convincing spectacle of him, but something about the
character will cause him to fail of entire conviction
and make the playwright appear just a trifle out of his
element. The Americans that Frenchmen or English-

men put into their plays are quite as curiously defective; even the American-experienced W. S. Maugham has, in "Our Betters," fumbled such a character in minor detail. Satisfactorily to handle a theme and a character, a playwright must have been born in the same house with them. Or at least next door.

§ 24

*Lost Scenes.*— It is one of the little tragedies of the American theatre that some of its finest dramatic scenes and episodes are forever lost to its history and to its records by virtue of the circumstance that they have appeared in generally inferior plays which have been quickly removed from the boards. The better plays, often without a single scene or episode so authentically vital, stimulating and moving, are preserved in book form, but the failures, with their occasional flash of fineness, are more often left to die forgotten and unmourned. Yet, as I have noted, in these failures — failures because the authors have been unable to make a single brilliant scene's vivid gleam spread its illumination fore and aft — we sometimes encounter dramatic jewels. There is room for a volume which will dig among the forgotten plays and extract from them and preserve their moments of authentic dazzle.

In such a volume there should be included the scene

in Harry Wagstaff Gribble's "Revolt," wherein the child evangelist, condescendingly patted on the head as a half-wit, suddenly turns upon her doubters and, with a world of innocent fervor, tears with her simple, ecstatic words into their hearts. There should also be the scene from Jim Tully's "Black Boy," one of the most dramatic ever shown on the stage, in which the nigger girl, tired of her black pugilistic lover and with the eyes of her heart already wandering to his black fighting rival, gradually hugs tighter and tighter to her breast the radio over which comes, round by round, the news of her erstwhile lover's slow but certain collapse under the blows of her heart's latest conqueror. There should be the laughing love scene from Harvey O'Higgins' and Harriet Ford's "Mr. Lazarus," one of the realest scenes of its kind in modern drama. And surely there should be the scene wherein the young girl, dreaming of the moon's wonder, takes leave of young Andrew Jackson on his way to fame and glory in the last act of Stallings' and Anderson's "First Flight."

Deserving of a place in the album of lost scenes is the one at the conclusion of Frederick Ballard's "Young America," wherein a run-over and wounded pet dog resolves, after everything else has failed, a family's acrimonious difficulties, to say nothing of the excellent comedy scene in Ben Hecht's "The Egotist" wherein the Lothario finds himself gradually bored to extinction by the elaborately seductive wiles of his latest feasible passion. Included also must be the scene between the two women and the bounder lover in Vincent Lawrence's "A Distant Drum"; the episode of the little chargirl's dumb bravery in disaster in Bertram Bloch's and Thomas Mitchell's "Glory Hallelujah"; the scene between Victoria and Albert in the "Queen Victoria" of David Carb and Walter Prichard Eaton; the scene of the young girl's defiance in Arthur Richman's "The Far Cry"; the scene between the two married couples in the second act of Lawrence's "Two Married Men," one of the most underestimated of American comedies; the scene between the degenerate youth Berchansky and the child Hagar in the last act of Dreiser's "The Hand of the Potter"; the scene between Edna, the prostitute fugitive from the law, and Little Red, the hobo, in Maxwell Anderson's dramatization of Tully's "Beggars of Life," known as "Outside Looking In"; and the scene between the woman and her maquereau in George Bronson Howard's and Wilson Mizner's "The Only Law." Also the scene of the theoretical hero's gradual self-betrayal in Gilbert Emery's "The Hero"; the scene at the piano in Hubert Osborne's dramatization of Julian Street's "Rita Coventry"; and the meeting of the old codgers in Edna Ferber's and George S. Kaufman's "Minick."

## § 25

*The Pirate Play.*— Some day someone will write a pirate play with a bit of originality to it, and if you think that will make me any happier you are mistaken. One of the things in the theatre that I have never been able to work up much excitement over is any kind of pirate play, whether first-class or fifth. And the reason is simple. Save they be set to music, pirates on the stage invariably look to me like a bad fancy-dress ball, and I find myself as unpersuaded by their loves and hates, their alarms and excursions, as I am by the gambols of any other gang of drunks. Stage pirates, though the playwright make them sober as judges, always seem a trifle inebriated. Whatever the nature of the play in which they are imbedded, there is generally a suggestion that they are pretty well liquored up. The error that the author usually makes is in allowing them the outward appearance of being half-seas-over and in permitting them contradictorily to speak like Prohibitionists. We are invariably treated to the same old troupe of actors dressed up like a road company of "Rio Rita"; the bold and swaggering La Tour who, despite his rough life on the buccaneering main, is always prettily barbered and modishly valeted; the governor's wife, Janice Waring, who, for all her cold, blonde beauty, is fetched by the bold fellow's glandular promise; the assistant villains, Diablo and Dominique; the bare-legged flapper with the cutlass at her side who accompanies the pirates on their cruises, evidently mistaking the Jolly Roger for the ensign of the Albany Night Boat; the boudoir scene in which the pirate chief seeks to deflower the proud beauty; and the grand finale in which, to an assortment of pirate college yells, love conquers all.

## § 26

*The College Play.*— Following the latter-day dramatic fashion, our playwrights have come to view life at the modern college as largely a matter of gin, road-houses and sex. In other days, these college plays centered upon the outcome of a football game, the hero of which was either an Indian in love with a rich New York débutante or a George Ade comedian in love with a college widow, or upon a boat race, the stroke of the winning crew greatly disconcerting the audience by resembling very closely a fairy. Today, however, all this is changed. Football, with its crowd of dollar-a-night supers sitting twenty feet above the stage level, their backs to the audience and yelling themselves hoarse over the tremendously exciting spectacle of a couple of stage-hands shooting craps on the imaginary gridiron, has given way to seduction, and crew races, which worked us all up to a high pitch, though they were presumably rowed in the six-foot space to the left of a tree at upper stage right, have similarly surrendered to carnal excursions.

## § 27

*The Guignol.*— Whenever the Grand Guignol in Paris is at a loss for a new way to give the visiting American drunks a thrill of horror, its management says to itself, "Oh what the hell, let's fall back on the old leper hokum." Accordingly, for the last twenty years plays have been produced every third month showing Mademoiselle Gaby Cocotte, the heartless jade, being made hideous for life, as punishment for her betrayal of the Mons. François Coucou, by the touch of the leprous Bush Wah, imported from India for the fell purpose by the vengeful François. While I am not much on figures, it is my guess that in the last two decades I have thus seen in the Rue Chaptal something like 1,310 faithless hussies contaminated by actors with white spots painted on their faces, 1,264 male loafers given the 50-50 by cast-off factory girls *via* leprosy germs sneaked into their *filet de bœuf Renaissance,* and something like twenty or thirty thousand American *kulaks* pleasurably electrified by the doings.

## § 28

*Monotony.*— The curse of the present English-

speaking stage is its monotony. With very rare exception, the minds of its playwrights run in droves and
it is only at great intervals that anything comes from
one of them that departs the stereotyped. The majority
of plays fall mechanically into definitely labeled
pigeon-holes and one is as much like another as the
reviews they perforce engender. It would be easy to
group the writers of these plays under exact produce
headings and just as easy to write reviews of their
plays in advance, qualifying them merely in unimportant detail. By way of illustration, run an eye over
the recent London stage and then over the current New
York platform. With the exception of a single British
exhibit and two American productions, nothing has
been shown in either theatre that does not fit itself
more or less neatly to a critical review prepared, out
of experience, in advance. In London as in New York
there have been the usual crook and mystery plays,
almost all of them as cut and dried as so many tobacco
leaves and varying only in the nature of their last
minute solutions and in the increasing badness of their
attempts at comedy relief. There have been the rubber-
stamp comedies of marital infelicity and sexual pec-
cadillo, all running close to formula and offering
originality only in the names of localities attributed to
the scenery and in the names of dressmakers credited
in the program. There are the usual younger generation to-dos, the usual Jewish salves, the usual adapta-

tions of lighter Continental comedies with the bour-
geois milieu and characters metamorphosed into
dandydom by way of tickling the snob box-office, and
the usual rewritings of their earlier themes by the more
conspicuous dramatists who have run out of inspira-
tion and fresh ideas.

Thus, to catalogue the Anglo-American playmakers,
we have such more distinguished members of the
card index as Shaw and Galsworthy delivering themselves of their fifteen-year-old ideas refurbished with
an occasionally new wheeze and such somewhat less
distinguished but sometimes estimable writers as
those of the drawing-room school revamping their
comedies of fifteen and twenty years ago only to the
extent of thinking up a new justification for sexual
divertissement on the part of their philandering husbands or wives. And thus, to catalogue further, we
have the posturers in profundity with their small
pieces of speculative pig-iron wrapped in reams of
tissue paper, the boys of the pistol school with their
childish jig-saw puzzles, the wisecracking corps with
their dramatized vaudeville sidewalk conversations,
and the assiduous strainers after novelty with their sub-
stitutions of arbitrary freakishness for imaginative
originality. Now and again there comes along a playwright with an adventuring mind and spirit and an
adventuring craftsmanship and idea, but the epiphany
is surely not a common one. For the most part, the

English and American stage of the moment is in the deadly hands of the cookie-cutters and paper-doll scissors wielders.

§ 29

*The New Hokum.*— With the relatively increased sophistication of theatre audiences, plainly apparent in several directions, it becomes evident that the long-established and hitherto prosperous dramatic hokum is on its last legs and that playwrights will very soon have to concoct new sure-fire devices if they wish to make certain of popular success. There is hardly a single one of the old hokum fetches that any longer gets its erstwhile positive reaction; instead, derision and laughter are the portion of the playwright who carelessly happens to indulge himself in them. Even the Cinderella story appears to have gone into the discard of popular theatre affection; once certain of success it today evokes inner hoots and open yawns. And the quondam hokum trinity, Mother, the Baby and the Flag, has been abandoned as futile and profitless even by such former shrewdly assiduous advocates as George M. Cohan. Mother love, long one of the best box-office bets, now save on rare occasions paves the way to Cain's storehouse and serves playwrights — as witness Sidney Howard's successful "The Silver Cord" — chiefly as a springboard whence to dive into irony. Babies, long good for sentimental snifflings, are now available only as material for low jest — as witness the successful "Little Accident" and "It's a Wise Child" — and the playwright who would dare to try to distil an audience's tears with one of them would only suffer ridicule. As for the Flag, one wave of it is enough to drive an audience away to the nearest English comedy or Frenchy farce.

The pistol from which the hero has covertly removed the bullets and with which the threatening villain once worked the audience up to a high state of suspense is presently as dead as the last three matches, two of them blown out in a critical situation and the last one, tremblingly nurtured, coming to flame to the audience's erstwhile nervous relief. The mysterious hand stealing around the portières and the sudden dousing of the lights now draw from an audience only a very impolite snicker. The smashing of a glass or window-pane that for thirty years was sure of an audience startle no longer works, nor does the sudden pistol shot. The villain bathed in a green light, the little child in a nightdress, the high-minded crook with a penchant for the old masters, the pulling of a handkerchief out of the hip pocket in lieu of a revolver, the sudden clap of thunder, the battering in of a door, the loud ticking of a clock, the dropped rose picked up wistfully by the hero, the blind orphan girl, the locket, the old and faithful darkey servant with lumbago, the playing of "Home, Sweet Home," the entrance of the Marines — such ancient hokums passed peacefully out of the theatre years ago. And, for all their greater and more stubborn persistence, dozens upon dozens of their kin are today rapidly following them into limbo.

The humorous hokum of the past is similarly dead wood so far as present-day audiences are concerned. The mere mention of a squirting dill-pickle or grape-fruit is now enough to bring forth a jeering howl. Stepping on a character's sore foot, getting the hand stuck in a decanter, a dismaying whack on the back under the guise of hearty approval, the defiant husband who, upon hearing his spouse call him, meekly puts his tail between his legs, the throwing of an imaginary object into the wings, whereupon a bell rings — to offer any one of them to an audience is to woo disaster. The hokum of long years' standing, whether dramatic or comic, has gone to the grave. The dawn of a new body of hokum that will galvanize our children and grandchildren is on its way.

§ 30

*A Suggestion.*— I have always wondered why it has never occurred to a producer to present Schnitzler's "Anatol" with a single actress playing each of the successive and various women's rôles. Each of Anatol's sweethearts is simply a different phase of the other, much as Leonora in Barrie's "The Legend of Leonora" is to her man seven or more women in one — an idea Barrie appropriated from Arsène Houssaye. True enough, this was not Schnitzler's idea when he wrote the play, but it would, with very little editing, improve the play and, more, give it the valuable continuity it now lacks. Furthermore, it would certainly improve its box-office value.

§ 31

*Russian Gloom.*— How the idea ever started that the Russian drama is indistinguishable from an undertaker's studio is pretty hard to make out, but it has enjoyed as long a life as any other fallacy concerned with American dramatic criticism. There is as much humor in the Slav drama as in any other, as the critics will discover if they will take the trouble carefully to scrutinize any number of such plays as Chekhov's "The Sea Gull" or "Uncle Vanya," Gorki's "Night Refuge," Erdman's "The Mandate," Turgenev's "A Month in the Country," Gogol's "The Inspector-General," Ostrovsky's "Not a Farthing" or "The Forest," Faiko's "Teacher Bubus," Griboyedov's "The Misfortune of Being Wise," Andreyev's "Savva," Evreinov's "The Theatre of the Soul," "The Merry Death" or "The Beautiful Despot," Artzybasheff's "Jealousy," Zamiatin's "The Flea," etc., etc.

## § 32

*Vaudeville.*— What has killed vaudeville as much as anything else, I suppose, is the departure of what may be called the vaudeville mood from life itself. The leisurely nonchalance, the caprice, the happy irresolution that blessed living in the America of another day have long since been drowned out by the loud whirr of the machine that has got most of us in its grip. Even among the rich, there is no leisure; there is only loafing. And the difference is readily graspable. A gentleman has leisure; a barbarian loafs. Taste, culture, experience and charm are essential to an appreciation and execution of leisure; loafing is the refuge of the unimaginative bounder. Vaudeville, like the vanished hansom cab, the window tables at Delmonico's and Sherry's, the four-hour lunches at Luchow's and checkers at the Lafayette, has paid the price of modern speed, money-grubbing and excited boredom. No longer is there time for such things; no longer are ease and casualness part of our lives; no longer are evenings to be sampled haphazardly. "Dinner at 7:30 sharp; the theatre at 8:50 sharp; the motor at 11:05 sharp; supper at 11:20 sharp" — life has become sharp, too sharp. Punctuality, once the privilege of princes, has become the command of stockbrokers. A cocktail, once a drink, has become a drug; and a dinner, once an event, has become an eventuality. Conversation has been supplanted by nervous wisecracks fighting against time, and love is made in taxicabs. Vaudeville was a symptom of the earlier dispensation, of a time and a year when there was place for boyish fun and simple nonsense and engaging unconcern. It was a kid game for men in their kid moments. And men don't seem to have such moments any more.

It is not that the old-time vaudeville show was a good show; it often, certainly, was anything but that. It was rather that it had an innocence and artlessness that made it appealing to men who prefer to take their diversion in a easy-come-easy-go fashion instead of in the railroad-schedule manner imposed upon them by present-day theatrical managers and traffic cops. That is the trouble with amusement in America under existing conditions. It has become a business where once it was a pleasure — and that is true not only of the theatre but of drinking, under the strictures of Prohibition; of reading, under the strictures of book-of-the-month clubs; of dancing, under the boiled-shirt and boiled-collar strictures of gunmen-operated night clubs; of eating, under the protein and vitamin strictures of quack dietitians; and of almost everything else, including what the poets call love. Vaudeville, whatever its asininity, was at least to be taken casually and the worse it was the more jocular it seemed to fellows who didn't mind throwing away a dollar but who currently object to throwing away six to see the same *Schuhplättler* and acrobats performing in front of a diamond revue curtain instead of in front of the good old drop of Union Square peopled by Pepsin Gum, Moe the Tailor and Root Beer advertisements. No one complains about a drugstore sandwich, because a drugstore sandwich is taken for granted. But anyone has a right to complain if one gets a drugstore sandwich at Café de Paris prices.

§ 33

*The Three Ideas.*— When the average writer of comedy is seized with an itch to be naughty, there are generally just three ideas that he is able to think up. The first is to get the wrong person into a bedroom; the second is to bring the hero and heroine as close as possible to a seduction; and the third is to combine the first two.

§ 34

*Music Show Titles.*— Whenever a musical show with a name like "Boom Boom" is produced, a lot of otherwise rational reviewers wax elaborately facetious over the employment of such titles for musical shows and plead for names with at least a little sense to them. Just why a show like "Boom Boom" shouldn't be called "Boom Boom," I can't make out. What would you call it if not by some such name as that? An exhibit consisting of two dozen jazz girls, a comedian who falls upon his seat and a scene in which the old Puritanical aunt from Boston gets drunk on gin punch would be untrue to any other kind of label. The best titles for such things are hardly, as the reviewers would seem to urge, "The Metaphysics of Maybelle," "Esmeralda Goes In For Epistemology," or "Up In Schopenhauer's Room," but "Piff, Paff, Pouf," "Criss-Cross," "Twinkle-Twinkle," "Whoopee" or "Boom Boom" — or some such nonsensical name as "Higgledy-Piggledy," "Fiddle-Dee-Doo," "Hoity-Toity" or "Twiddle-Twaddle" which used to fit the situation perfectly in the old Weber and Fields days.

## § 35

*La Langue Verte.*— Ever since the authors of "What Price Glory?" freed American dramatic language of certain of its inhibitions, we have engaged playwrights who have sought to mimic their success. Most of these cuckoos, however, have simply mimicked the language without making it an honest and integral part of the plays and characters that exuded it. As a result, we have had a series of exhibitions that have tried to pass themselves off as strong meat on the ground of their cursing alone, much as inarticulate weaklings seek to suggest strength by recourse to an absurd and incongruous Billingsgate. The business has gone so far, indeed, that a *God damn* today hasn't half so much force in the theatre as a simple *Oh*. It has turned upon itself and become caricature. Little Orphant Annies have so often been made arbitrarily to shout *Bastard*, Our Nell has so regularly been forced to take the Saviour's name in vain, and allusions to the male off-spring of female dogs, equine posteriors, the W.C. and I.H.S. have become so common that longshore-men have been driven to the flea circus for a little genteel relief.

## § 36

*The Other Niche.*— In the minds of most critics there are two niches wherein linger the memories of two groups of plays; in one, the memories of the un-deniably great and, in the other, the memories of the deniably great but nonetheless immensely enchanting. I am not at all sure, indeed, that these less august plays do not often perfume the recollection more pungently than some of the established classics. Who, by way of example, can ever quite forget Fulda's "Friends of Our Youth," or Brieux's "Les Hanne-tons," or Rostand's "Last Night of Don Juan," or Meyer-Förster's "Old Heidelberg," or Barrie's "The Legend of Leonora," or de Caillavet's, de Flers' and Arène's "The King," or Dunsany's "Laughter of the

Gods" and "A Good Bargain," or Birmingham's "General John Regan," or Jerome K. Jerome's "The Great Gamble" (at least the beginning and the end), or Henry Arthur Jones' "Joseph Entangled" and "The Case of Rebellious Susan," or Lennox Robinson's "Patriots" and "The White-Headed Boy," or Schnitzler's "Christmas Presents," or Chesterton's "Magic," or Molnar's "The Swan" and "The Glass Slipper," or Bahr's "The Master," or Schönherr's "Children's Tragedy," or Hubert Henry Davies' "A Single Man," — or a number of other such plays still regarded with some skepticism by the scholarly professors?

§ 37

*The Dramatized Novel.*— While a cheap and commonplace novel may, I suppose, be dramatized and exhibited on the stage without damage either to the cheap, commonplace novel or to the cheaper and more commonplace customers of such theatrical stuffs, a reputable novel no more lends itself to completely satisfying drama than a reputable painting does to a completely satisfying lithograph. That, indeed, is what even the best novel dramatizations are: dramatic lithographs. They catch the external look and color of the original; they catch the scene and even some of the mood; but they fail to catch what never can be caught, to wit, that technical exactitude and precision of essence which makes a work of art what it is and which can no more be unblurringly duplicated in a second-hand copy than the clear, sharp outline of a typewriter's script can be caught by a carbon. Every art is a law unto itself and the borderlands between them are treacherous with difficult mountain passes and sinister gulleys. The occasional bridges joining one with another are at best rickety and dubious and result only in such triumphs of bastardy as talking moving pictures, grand opera and interpretative dancing. The dramatized novel thus takes its place alongside the novelized drama. Both are anomalies, freaks: robots in falseface, two distinct arts Siamesed with boloney skins.

## § 38

*Dirty Plays.*— To a good dirty play that comes unabashed into the open, I have no objection; in point of fact, I sometimes enjoy such an exhibit hugely; my gleeful chuckles can be heard ten blocks away. But these masked dirty plays have the same effect upon me that a smoking-car story has when it is told by a money-soliciting clergyman. They are not forthright in their dirt but laboriously sneaky, like an old man who, at a supper party, puts his hand on the knee of the young woman seated next to him under the pretence that he is feeling around for his dropped napkin.

## § 39

*American Farce.*— The student of American theatrical phenomena gradually finds himself impressed with one fact, namely, that however low the status of the more serious native drama may be, the native farce is not only often a thing of considerable quality but just as often superior to any farce writing currently being done abroad. In Europe, farce usually is made to concern itself for the most part with the various ramifications of amour, chiefly illicit. Save for the occasional injection into it, in France, of an actor dressed up to represent a member of the Chamber of Deputies or, in Germany, of one described as the mayor of a provincial town, it has negligible contact with life and the world outside the boudoir. Its humorous commentary is directed not against public affairs so much as against love affairs and the result is an unbroken succession of spectacles concerned with infidelity, adultery, the sudden and unexpected return of husbands and the hiding of lovers under or in the bed. There was a day, during the period of such playwrights as de Caillavet and de Flers in France and such as Fulda in Germany, when farce or the more boisterous comedy treated satirically of events and conditions more acute and lively, but that day is apparently done. What is true of the Continent is also true of England; the farce writing that is being negotiated there at present is simply the French kind of thing puritanically bowdlerized.

In America, on the contrary, there is observable an increasing tendency to break away from the old anatomical farce and to confect a farce that in one way or another shall reflect critically upon the idiosyncrasies of the national life and its various enterprises. "Break away" is perhaps not a happy phrase, for the tendency has been noticeable since the era of Charles H. Hoyt and his farces that scratched drolly the epidermis of congressmen, civic organizations, stuffed-shirt military orders and other items in the humorous Americana of his time. Since the very beginnings of American farce, indeed, this interest in public as against mere boudoir bizarreries has often been strikingly evident. Fashionable society as American British-apes exhibit it, American advertising, American newspapers, American politics, American municipal administration, American hypocrisy, American money-madness, American business — such subjects have been the food of American farce and as a consequence the latter has frequently proved to be the most stimulating, corrective and derisorily tonic page in the native dramatic catalogue. I am not certain, indeed, that American farce is not, by and large, the best and most important contribution that America has made to its own theatre. In it there has been a keener and more recognizably pointed appraisal and criticism of American life, enterprise and manners than in all the more serious plays which that theatre has shown.

The farces of Hoyt — not to go back too far and resolve this dossier into a mere burdensome catalogue, the farces of Ade and Cohan and Megrue, the farces of Hecht and McArthur, Maurine Watkins, Lardner and Kaufman, or Kaufman and seemingly any other man he elects as his playwriting partner are among the real treasures of the scantily stocked American dramatic chest. They have held the mirror up to American institutions, pretensions and imbecilities as has no other species of drama. They have been the castor oil of a nation that has need of a lot of it.

There is a type of critical mind that disparages farce as a low dramatic form. With melodrama, it is relegated to the cellar of dramatic art. Yet farce, like melodrama, often resolves itself into the finest funnel of dramatic purpose. It is, or at least in imaginative, intelligent and expert hands it may be, the best antidote to an institution's, a people's or a nation's posturings and vainglory. It is a policeman in cap and bells, and with a papier-mâché club filled with lead. It criticizes with a laugh what can never so effectively be criticized with a frown. It is the professorial drama with a salutary tack self-deposited upon its own chair.

§ 40

*The Showshop Forlorn.*— One of the major troubles

with the American theatre today is that, even when what it offers on its stage is worthwhile, the theatre itself is an unappetizing place. Once an establishment as brilliantly lit up as a sailor on shore leave, once patronized by a gay and glamourous crowd, once an element in the social life of the community, it has in late years fallen upon dark and dull days until presently — with very few exceptions — it physically possesses all the allure of a colored washerwoman.

What the theatre needs even more than good plays is that air of radiance and picnic that it used to have and that it has now only on rare occasions. The movie people have profited by the theatre's more recent slovenliness and have cozened trade from it by dolling up their film parlors like so many servant girls on St. Patrick's Day. Where the theatres presently economize on fancy electric illumination, the movie bordellos go the whole hog and draw in the passersby with fronts that look like an explosion in a Mexican diamond mine. Where the dramatic houses shrink into the side-streets, as if they had been caught stealing jam and were afraid of being spanked, the screen cabarets throw out their chests along the main thoroughfares and *dare* anyone to try to get in, emphasizing the dare with long lines of jakes fighting to elbow their way to the ticket-window. And where the theatres, once you get inside them, offer the aspect of a Flatbush sitting-room, only not so clean, the cinema palazzos offer interiors indistinguishable from a marriage of the *Ile de France* and the old Silver Dollar saloon.

The majority of people, when they go to a theatre, want a theatre that looks like a theatre and feels like a theatre and smells like a theatre, not an ex-garage with a few hundred chairs in it that looks, feels and smells like an ex-garage. And that is what such customers for the most part get when they go to the theatre today. One of the reasons for the success of theatres like the New Amsterdam is surely the circumstance that they are theatres in every sense of the word and not merely brownstone-fronts or Italian restaurants converted into theatres by printing the word *Asbestos* on a cotton drop-curtain and hiring a frowzy woman to show you to an uncomfortable seat. It is true that the New Amsterdam, to name but one of the real theatres, generally houses pretty good shows, but I have a feeling that if these same shows were put on in any one of a dozen less authentic theatres they would not draw half the trade that they draw in the house in question.

Every once in a while, one of the pseudo-theatres playing a dramatic attraction becomes conscious of its absurd pose as a theatre and tries to put itself over on its customers by installing a couple of guitar players in one of the boxes or by redecorating its side walls to look like bargain day in Wanamaker's wall-paper department. But it fools nobody. The dodges only make its pretence of being a theatre the more obvious and ridiculous. A theatre, after all, must be a theatre from the moment its plans leave the architect's hands and from the moment its doors are first opened. And many of our theatres are theatres only by after-thought. They have stages, true enough, and their chairs are arranged in rows and are numbered, and programs announcing on the covers that they are theatres are handed around, but they are actually and essentially no more theatres than so many hinterland town-halls. Even the two guitar players have to laugh at them.

## GEORGE JEAN NATHAN

*has been an ardent observer of the theatre ever since his undergraduate days at Cornell University where he took an active part in college dramatics. After a year at the University of Bologna, he joined the editorial staff of* THE NEW YORK HERALD *(1905-1906). Since then his writings both as dramatic critic for such magazines as* HARPER'S WEEKLY, PUCK *(with James Huneker),* SMART SET, JUDGE *and* THE AMERICAN MERCURY, *and as author of many books on the theatre have made him the most widely read, the most widely known, the most widely imitated and the most widely discussed critic of the theatre in this country. With H. L. Mencken, he edited* SMART SET *from 1914 to 1923 and founded* THE AMERICAN MERCURY *in 1924. At present Mr. Nathan devotes most of his time to his books and to his work as dramatic editor of* VANITY FAIR.

THIS BOOK WAS SET ON THE LINOTYPE
IN BODONI, ELECTROTYPED, PRINTED
AND BOUND BY H. WOLFF ESTATE,
NEW YORK. THE PAPER WAS
MADE BY W. C. HAMILTON
& SONS, MIQUON, PA.